Inside Reading

THE ACADEMIC WORD LIST IN CONTEXT

By Arline Burgmeier
Series Director: Cheryl Boyd Zimmerman

1

OXFORD
UNIVERSITY PRESS

OXFORD
UNIVERSITY PRESS

198 Madison Avenue
New York, NY 10016 USA

Great Clarendon Street, Oxford OX2 6DP UK

Oxford University Press is a department of the University of Oxford.
It furthers the University's objective of excellence in research, scholarship,
and education by publishing worldwide in

Oxford   New York

Auckland Cape Town Dar es Salaam Hong Kong Karachi
Kuala Lumpur Madrid Melbourne Mexico City Nairobi
New Delhi Shanghai Taipei Toronto

With offices in

Argentina Austria Brazil Chile Czech Republic France Greece
Guatemala Hungary Italy Japan Poland Portugal Singapore
South Korea Switzerland Thailand Turkey Ukraine Vietnam

OXFORD and OXFORD ENGLISH are registered trademarks of
Oxford University Press.

© Oxford University Press 2009

Database right Oxford University Press (maker)

Library of Congress Cataloging-in-Publication Data
Burgmeier, Arline
    Inside reading 1: the academic word list in context / Arline Burgmeier.
        p. cm.
    ISBN 978-0-19-441612-2 (pbk. w/ cdrom)
    1. English language—Textbooks for foreign speakers. 2. Vocabulary. I. Title.
PE1128.B846 2007
    428.2'4—dc22   2007023406

No unauthorized photocopying.

Editorial Director: Sally Yagan
Senior Managing Editor: Patricia O'Neill
Editor: Dena Daniel
Design Director: Robert Carangelo
Design Manager: Maj-Britt Hagsted
Production Artist: Julie Armstrong
Compositor: TSI Graphics Inc.
Cover design: Stacy Merlin
Manufacturing Manager: Shanta Persaud
Manufacturing Controller: Eve Wong

Student book pack ISBN: 978 0 19 441612 2

Student book ISBN: 978 0 19 441600 9

Printed in Hong Kong

10 9 8 7 6 5 4 3 2 1

ACKNOWLEDGMENTS

The publisher would like to thank TSI Graphics for the illustrations used in this book.

*The publisher would like to thank the following for their permission to reproduce
photographs:* Key Color/Jupiter Images: 3; Vintage Images/Getty Images: 3;
Ilene MacDonald/Alamy: 8; Greenshoots Communications/Alamy: 16; North
Wind Picture Archives: 23; James Quine/Alamy: 30; Adrian Sherratt/Alamy: 44;
Comstock Images/Alamy: 51; Ablestock/Jupiter Images: 52; Walker Art Gallery,
National Museums Liverpool/ The Bridgeman Art Library Nationality: 64;
The Granger Collection, New York: 78; Brand X Pictures/ Jupiter Images: 79; Tim
Boyle/Getty Images: 86; George Marks / Getty Images: 92; Peter Horree / Alamy:
93; Henry Groskinsky/Time & Life Pictures/Getty Images: 120; Pet/Getty Images
128; Win McNamee/Getty Images: 136.

Cover art: Imagemore / Getty Images: Tropical Fish; Photodisc / C Squared
Studios / Age FotoStock: Bicycle

The publisher would like to thank the following for their help: "Top 50 Franchises, by
Number of Franchises, 2005," Entreprenuer, Jan. 2006. Data from figure "A Loo
at Who Does the Most Fishing," from Unmesh Kher, "Oceans of Nothing," Time
Nov. 13, 2006, pp. 57, 58.

*The author would like to acknowledge several particularly valuable sources of information
incorporated into the articles and activities of this textbook:* Unit 2: Centers for Disease
Control and Prevention website; Medical Museum: University of Iowa Health
Care website; Unit 3: The 22 Immutable Laws of Marketing by Al Ries and
Jack Trout; Strategic Name Development website; Unit 6: The Casebook of
Forensic Detection by Colin Evans; Popular Science; Unit 7: Fast Food Nation by
Eric Schlosser; Franchise Council of Australia website; Unit 10: Rehabilitation
Institute of Chicago website. The author would also like to acknowledge Los
Angeles Times and Time for countless articles that provided up-to-the-minute
information on many of the topics discussed in the textbook.

Acknowledgments

From the Series Director

Inside Reading represents collaboration as it should be. That is, the project resulted from a balance of expertise from a team at Oxford University Press (OUP) and a collection of skilled participants from several universities. The project would not have happened without considerable investment and talent from both sides.

This idea took root and developed with the collaboration and support of the OUP editorial team. I am particularly grateful to Pietro Alongi, whose vision for this series began with his recognition of the reciprocal relationship between reading and vocabulary. I am also grateful to Dena Daniel, the lead editor on the project, and Janet Aitchison for her involvement in the early stages of this venture.

OUP was joined by the contributions of participants from various academic settings. First, Averil Coxhead, Massey University, New Zealand, created the Academic Word List, a principled, research-based collection of academic words which has led both to much of the research which supports this project and to the materials themselves. Dr. Tom Klammer, Dean of Humanities and Social Sciences at California State University, Fullerton (CSUF), made my participation in this project possible, first by endorsing its value, then by providing the time I needed. Assistance and insight were provided by CSUF participants Patricia Balderas, Arline Burgmeier, and Margaret Plenert, as well as by many TESOL Masters students at CSUF.

Finally, thank you to the many reviewers who gave us feedback along the way: Nancy Baum, **University of Texas at Arlington**; Adele Camus, **George Mason University**; Carole Collins, **Northampton Community College**; Jennifer Farnell, **University of Connecticut**, ALP; Laurie Frazier, **University of Minnesota**; Debbie Gold, **California State University**, Long Beach, ALI; Janet Harclerode and Toni Randall, **Santa Monica Community College**; Marianne Hsu Santelli, **Middlesex County College**; Steve Jones, **Community College of Philadelphia**; Lucille King, **University of Connecticut**; Shalle Leeming, **Academy of Art University**, San Francisco; Gerry Luton, **University of Victoria**; David Mindock, **University of Denver**; William Morrill, **University of Washington**; and Peggy Alptekin. This is collaboration indeed!

From the Author

I would like to thank my dear friend Cheryl Zimmerman for encouraging me to undertake this project; and for endlessly nurturing my affinity with second language vocabulary teaching and learning. My thanks also go to Oxford University Press editor Dena Daniel for her guidance while getting started, and for her insight and experience in polishing the finished product. Special thanks go to my daughter, Diane Dantas, whose diary entries about her autistic son, Sean, inspired the narrative about "Shawn" used in this book.

Contents

To the Teacher

There is a natural relationship between academic reading and word learning. *Inside Reading* is a four-level reading and vocabulary series designed to use this relationship to best advantage. Through principled instruction and practice with reading strategies and skills, students will increase their ability to comprehend reading material. Likewise, through a principled approach to the complex nature of vocabulary knowledge, learners will better understand how to make sense of the complex nature of academic word learning. *Inside Reading 1* is intended for students at the low-intermediate level.

Academic Reading and Vocabulary: A Reciprocal Relationship

In the beginning stages of language learning, when the learner is making simple connections between familiar oral words and written forms, vocabulary knowledge plays a crucial role. In later stages, such as those addressed by *Inside Reading*, word learning and reading are increasingly interdependent: rich word knowledge facilitates reading, and effective reading skills facilitate vocabulary comprehension and learning.[1]

The word knowledge that is needed by the reader in this reciprocal process is more than knowledge of definitions.[2] Truly knowing a word well enough to use it in reading (as well as in production) means knowing something about its grammar, word forms, collocations, register, associations, and a great deal about its meaning, including its connotations and multiple meanings.[3] Any of this information may be called upon to help the reader make the inferences needed to understand the word's meaning in a particular text. For example, a passage's meaning can be controlled completely by a connotation

She was *frugal*. (positive connotation)

She was *stingy*. (negative connotation)

by grammatical form

He valued his *memory*.

He valued his *memories*.

or an alternate meaning

The *labor* was intense. (physical work vs. childbirth)

Inside Reading recognizes the complexity of knowing a word. Students are given frequent and varied practice with all aspects of word knowledge. Vocabulary activities are closely related in topic to the reading selections, providing multiple exposures to a word in actual use and opportunities to work with its meanings, grammatical features, word forms, collocations, register, and associations.

To join principled vocabulary instruction with academic reading instruction is both natural and effective. *Inside Reading* is designed to address the reciprocal relationship between reading and vocabulary and to use it to help students develop academic proficiency.

A Closer Look at Academic Reading

Students preparing for academic work benefit from instruction that includes attention to the language as well as attention to the process of reading. The Interactive Reading model indicates that reading is an active process in which readers draw upon *top-down processing* (bringing meaning to the text), as well as *bottom-up processing* (decoding words and other details of language).[4]

The *top-down* aspect of this construct suggests that reading is facilitated by interesting and relevant reading materials that activate a range of knowledge in a reader's mind, knowledge that is refined and extended during the act of reading.

The *bottom-up* aspect of this model suggests that the learner needs to pay attention to language proficiency, including vocabulary. An academic reading course must address the teaching of higher-level reading strategies without neglecting the need for language support.[5]

---

[1] Koda, 2005

[2] See the meta-analysis of L1 vocabulary studies by Stahl & Fairbanks, 1986.

[3] Nation, 1990

[4] Carrell, Devine and Eskey, 1988

[5] Birch, 2002; Eskey, 1988

Inside Reading addresses both sides of the interactive model. High-interest academic readings and activities provide students with opportunities to draw upon life experience in their mastery of a wide variety of strategies and skills, including

- previewing
- scanning
- using context clues to clarify meaning
- finding the main idea
- summarizing
- making inferences.

Rich vocabulary instruction and practice that targets vocabulary from the Academic Word List (AWL) provide opportunities for students to improve their language proficiency and their ability to decode and process vocabulary.

A Closer Look at Academic Vocabulary

Academic vocabulary consists of those words which are used broadly in all academic domains, but are not necessarily frequent in other domains. They are words in the academic register that are needed by students who intend to pursue higher education. They are not the technical words used in one academic field or another (e.g., *genetics, fiduciary, proton*), but are found in all academic areas, often in a supportive role (*substitute, function, inhibit*).

The most principled and widely accepted list of academic words to date is The Academic Word List (AWL), compiled by Averil Coxhead in 2000. Its selection was based on a corpus of 3.5 million words of running text from academic materials across four academic disciplines: the humanities, business, law, and the physical and life sciences. The criteria for selection of the 570 word families on the AWL was that the words appear frequently and uniformly across a wide range of academic texts, and that they not appear among the first 2000 most common words of English, as identified by the General Service List.[6]

Across the four levels of *Inside Reading*, students are introduced to the 570 word families of the AWL

at a gradual pace of about 15 words per unit. Their usage is authentic, the readings in which they appear are high interest, and the words are practiced and recycled in a variety of activities, facilitating both reading comprehension and word learning.

There has been a great deal of research into the optimal classroom conditions for facilitating word learning. This research points to several key factors.

Noticing: Before new words can be learned, they must be noticed. Schmidt, in his well-known *noticing hypothesis*, states

> noticing is the necessary and sufficient condition for converting input into intake. Incidental learning, on the other hand, is clearly both possible and effective when the demands of a task focus attention on what is to be learned.[7]

Inside Reading facilitates noticing in two ways. Target words are printed in boldface type at their first occurrence to draw the students' attention to their context, usage, and word form. Students are then offered repeated opportunities to focus on them in activities and discussions. *Inside Reading* also devotes activities and tasks to particular target words. This is often accompanied by a presentation box giving information about the word, its family members, and its usage.

Teachers can further facilitate noticing by preteaching selected words through "rich instruction," meaning instruction that focuses on what it means to know a word, looks at the word in more than one setting, and involves learners in actively processing the word.[8] *Inside Reading* facilitates rich instruction by providing engaging activities that use and spotlight target words in both written and oral practice.

Repetition: Word learning is incremental. A learner is able to pick up new knowledge about a word with each encounter. Repetition also assists learner memory—multiple exposures at varying intervals dramatically enhance retention.

Repetition alone doesn't account for learning; the types and intervals of repetitions are also important.

---

6 West, 1953; Coxhead 2000
7 Schmidt, 1990, p. 129
8 Nation, 2001, p. 157

Research shows that words are best retained when the practice with a new word is brief but the word is repeated several times at increasing intervals.[9] *Inside Reading* provides multiple exposures to words at varying intervals and recycles vocabulary throughout the book to assist this process.

Learner involvement: Word-learning activities are not guaranteed to be effective simply by virtue of being interactive or communicative. Activities or tasks are most effective when learners are most *involved* in them. Optimal involvement is characterized by a learner's own perceived need for the unknown word, the desire to search for the information needed for the task, and the effort expended to compare the word to other words. It has been found that the greater the level of learner involvement, the better the retention.[10]

The activities in *Inside Reading* provide opportunities to be involved in the use of target words at two levels:

- "Word level," where words are practiced in isolation for the purpose of focusing on such aspects as meaning, derivation, grammatical features, and associations.
- "Sentence level," where learners respond to the readings by writing and paraphrasing sentences.

Because the activities are grounded in the two high-interest readings of each unit, they provide the teacher with frequent opportunities to optimize learner involvement.

Instruction and practice with varying types of word knowledge: To know a word means to know a great deal about the word.[11] The activities in this book include practice with all aspects of word knowledge: form (both oral and written), meaning, multiple meanings, collocations, grammatical features, derivatives, register, and associations.

Helping students become independent word learners: No single course or book can address all of the words a learner will need. Students should leave a class with new skills and strategies for word learning so that they can notice and effectively practice new words as they encounter them. *Inside Reading* includes several features to help guide students to becoming independent word learners. One is a self-assessment activity, which begins and ends each unit. Students evaluate their level of knowledge of each word, ranging from not knowing a word at all, to word recognition, and then to two levels of word use. This exercise demonstrates the incremental nature of word knowledge, and guides learners toward identifying what they know and what they need to know. Students can make better progress if they accurately identify the aspects of word knowledge they need for themselves. Another feature is the use of references and online resources: To further prepare students to be independent word learners, instruction and practice in dictionary use and online resources are provided throughout the book.

The *Inside Reading* Program

Inside Reading offers students and teachers helpful ancillaries:

Student CD-ROM: The CD-ROM in the back of every student book contains additional practice activities for students to work with on their own. The activities are self-correcting and allow students to redo an activity as many times as they wish.

Instructor's pack: The Instructor's pack contains the answer key for the book along with a test generator CD-ROM. The test generator contains one test per student book unit. Each test consists of a reading passage related to the topic of the unit, which features the target vocabulary. This is followed by reading comprehension and vocabulary questions. Teachers can use each unit's test in full or customize it in a variety of ways.

Inside Reading optimizes the reciprocal relationship between reading and vocabulary by drawing upon considerable research and many years of teaching experience. It provides the resources to help students read well and to use that knowledge to develop both a rich academic vocabulary and overall academic language proficiency.

---

[9] Research findings are inconclusive about the number of repetitions that are needed for retention. Estimates range from 6 to 20. See Nation, 2001, for a discussion of repetition and learning.

[10] Laufer & Hulstijn, 2001

[11] Nation, 1990; 2001

References

Carrel, P.L., Devine, J., & Eskey, D.E. (1988). *Interactive approaches to second language reading*. Cambridge: Cambridge University Press. (Or use "Holding in the bottom" by Eskey)

Coxhead, A. (2000). A new academic word list. *TESOL Quarterly, 34*, 213-238.

Eskey, D.E. (1988). Holding in the bottom. In P.L. Carrel, J. Devine, & D.E. Eskey, *Interactive approaches to second language reading,* pp. 93-100. Cambridge: Cambridge University Press.

Koda, K. (2005). *Insights into second language reading*. Cambridge: Cambridge University Press.

Laufer, B. (2005). Instructed second language vocabulary learning: The fault in the 'default hypothesis'. In A. Housen & M. Pierrard (Eds.), *Investigations in Instructed Second Language Acquisition,* pp. 286-303. New York: Mouton de Gruyter.

Laufer, B. (1992). Reading in a foreign language: How does L2 lexical knowledge interact with the reader's general academic ability? *Journal of Research in Reading, 15*(2), 95-103.

Nation, I.S.P. (1990). *Teaching and learning vocabulary*. New York: Newbury House.

Nation, I.S.P. (2001). *Learning vocabulary in another language*. Cambridge: Cambridge University Press.

Schmidt, R. (1990). The role of consciousness in second language learning. *Applied Linguistics, 11,* 129-158.

Schmitt, N. (2000). *Vocabulary in language teaching*. Cambridge: Cambridge University Press.

Schmitt, N. & Zimmerman, C.B. (2002). Derivative word forms: What do learners know? *TESOL Quarterly, 36*(2), 145-171.

Stahl, S.A. & Fairbanks, M.M. (1986). The effects of vocabulary instruction: A model-based meta-analysis. *Review of Educational Research, 56*(1), 72-110.

Welcome to *Inside Reading*

Inside Reading is a four-level series that develops students' abilities to interact with and access academic reading and vocabulary, preparing them for success in the academic classroom.

There are ten units in *Inside Reading*. Each unit features two readings on a high-interest topic from an academic content area, one or more reading skills and strategies, and work with a set of target word families from the **Academic Word List**.

UNIT OPENER

Unit
6
Science

SOLVING CRIMES WITH SCIENCE

In this unit, you will

- ➲ read about the use of science to solve crimes.
- ➲ learn to identify time and sequence words.
- ➲ increase your understanding of the target academic words for this unit:

authority	contrary	instance	panel	tape
conclude	detect	logic	site	technical
consult	establish	motive	specific	

SELF-ASSESSMENT OF TARGET WORDS

Think carefully about how well you know each target word in this unit. Then, write it in the appropriate column in the chart.

I have never seen the word before.	I have seen the word but am not sure what it means.	I understand the word when I see or hear it in a sentence.	I have tried to use this word, but I am not sure I am using it correctly.	I use the word with confidence in either speaking *or* writing.	I use the word with confidence, both in speaking *and* writing.

MORE WORDS YOU'LL NEED

detective: a person, usually a police officer, who helps solve crimes

evidence: signs or proof that something exists or is true

suspect: a person that police believe may have committed a crime

SOLVING CRIMES WITH SCIENCE **71**

The opening page of each unit introduces the **content area** and **topic**.

The unit's **goals** and **target academic vocabulary** are presented so that students can start to think about their knowledge of the topic and focus on the reading strategies and target word families they will deal with in the unit.

Each unit starts with a **self-assessment activity** to heighten student awareness of their own word knowledge. Students will come back to this activity at the end of the unit to re-assess their knowledge and evaluate their progress.

NOTE

Inside Reading is designed so that units can be taught in order or randomly, depending on students' needs.

READING 1

BEFORE YOU READ

Read these questions. Discuss your answers in a small group.

1. Do you ever watch crime stories on television? If so, which one is your favorite?
2. Why do you think people like movies, TV programs, or books about solving crimes?
3. What are some ways that science can help the police solve crimes?

READ

This newspaper article tells the story of how the police solved the case of a mysterious death.

Solving a Crime with Science: A True Story

On the morning of June 11, 1986, Sue Snow woke up with a headache. She took two Extra-Strength Excedrin capsules and within minutes she collapsed to the floor. She was rushed to a
5 hospital, but died hours later.

Doctors were unable to explain Sue's death. They asked the hospital laboratory to do some tests to **establish** the cause. One test **detected** cyanide, a poison that can rapidly kill a person
10 who swallows even a small amount. The hospital immediately called the police. They began their investigation by interviewing members of Sue's family.

Mrs. Snow's daughter recalled that her mother
15 had a headache the morning she died and that she had taken two Extra-Strength Excedrin capsules. When a police laboratory subsequently

the two **sites** but learned nothing. Through the
30 media, they warned people about the poisoned medicine and asked them to phone if they had any useful information.

Six days after Sue Snow's death, a woman named Stella Nickell phoned the police to
35 report that her husband, Bruce, had died suddenly on June 5 after taking Extra-Strength Excedrin capsules. When the police searched Stella Nickell's house, they found two bottles of poisoned Extra-Strength Excedrin capsules.

40 A police detective thought something was very odd. The crime laboratory had tested over 740,000 Extra-Strength Excedrin capsules and found poisoned capsules in only five bottles: two from sites in nearby towns, one in Sue
45 Snow's house and two in Stella Nickell's house. Mrs. Nickell claimed that she had bought her two bottles at two different stores on two different days. **Contrary** to what she claimed,

---

Before each of the two readings in a unit, students discuss questions to **activate knowledge of the specific topic** dealt with in the reading.

Readings represent **a variety of genres**: newspapers, magazines, websites, press releases, encyclopedias, and books.

Target vocabulary is bold at its first occurrence to aid recognition. **Vocabulary is recycled** and practiced throughout the unit. Target words are also recycled in subsequent units.

READING COMPREHENSION

Reading comprehension questions follow each text to check students' understanding and recycle target vocabulary.

READING COMPREHENSION

Mark each sentence as *T* (True) or *F* (False) according to the information in Reading 2. Use your dictionary to check the meaning of new words.

.... 1. Holmes inspected a crime site for anything related to the crime, for instance footprints, broken glass, or hair.

.... 2. CSIs are part of a panel of technical experts in a forensic investigation.

.... 3. Forensic laboratories establish when and where a murder took place by taking hundreds of photographs.

.... 4. To identify footprints, forensic laboratories consult files of footprints of known criminals.

.... 5. CSIs use handheld magnifying glasses to detect trace evidence at crime scenes.

.... 6. Authorities have contrary opinions about using fingerprints for identification.

.... 7. DNA analysis can conclusively establish the motive for a crime.

.... 8. Samples of a suspect's voice can be compared to voice samples from

READING STRATEGIES

Strategy presentation and practice accompanies each reading.

READING STRATEGY: Identifying Time and Sequence Words

Understanding the *order of events* in a story is often essential for understanding the story, especially a mystery such as Reading 1. The order of events can be shown in several ways:

1. Sentences in a paragraph usually describe actions in the order that they happened.
2. Time words such as *Monday, March, summer*, or *1987* tell when actions took place.
3. Words such as *before, after, soon, first, next, meanwhile, then, finally*, and *subsequently* can show the order of events.
4. Phrases such as *three days later, the next year*, and *at the same time* also show time order.

A. Use time clues in the reading to determine the date of each of these events.

Sue Snow died ....

Bruce Nickell died ....

Stella Nickell phoned the police ....

VOCABULARY ACTIVITIES

The vocabulary work following each reading **starts at word level**. Step I activities are mostly receptive and focus on meanings and word family members.

STEP I VOCABULARY ACTIVITIES: Word Level

A. Use the target vocabulary in the box to complete this story. The words in parentheses can help you.

abandon	expand	inclined
acknowledges	generations	rejecting
albeit	in contrast	

The people of past .... ate in restaurants only on weekends or
(1. *people born at about the same time*)
special occasions. ...., people today are .... to eat
(2. *showing a difference*) (3. *likely*)
out several times a week. This could be a problem if their menu choice is always a
hamburger and French fries. Nearly everyone .... that too much
(4. *agrees that it's true*)
fat in the diet is not healthy. Unfortunately, hamburgers and French fries are high
in fat, ... delicious. Instead of .... fast food
(5. *although*) (6. *refusing*)
altogether, people should simply .... the burgers and fries and
(7. *stop having*)
.... their food choices by ordering something different.
(8. *increase*)

Vocabulary work then **progresses to the sentence level**. Step II activities are mostly productive and feature work with collocations and specific word usage. These activities can also include work with register, associations, connotations, and learner dictionaries.

STEP II VOCABULARY ACTIVITIES: Sentence Level

To *expand* means "to grow or increase." The noun form is *expansion*. The adjective form is *expansive*. It means "to cover a wide area."

The **expansion** took nearly a year to complete.

People are happy with the **expansive** new parking lot at the store.

E. Restate these sentences in your notebook, using the form of *expand* in parentheses.

1. The McDonald's menu now includes salads. (*has expanded*)
2. By 2002, the network of McDonald's franchises covered 120 foreign countries. (*expansive*)
3. Recently, McDonald's growth has been faster overseas than in the U.S. (*has been expanding*)
4. Many McDonald's franchises have added a children's play yard to increase their appeal to families. (*expand*)

NOTE

Each unit ends with topics and projects that teachers can use to take the lesson further. This section includes class discussion topics, online research projects, and essay ideas.

Unit 1

Engineering

RIDING THROUGH HISTORY

In this unit, you will

⮕ read about two very different vehicles and how they were created.

⮕ learn how to preview a text to improve your reading comprehension.

⮕ increase your understanding of the target academic words for this unit:

alter	framework	injure	overseas	subsequent
design	individual	job	primary	substitute
fee	inherent	minimize	revolution	

SELF-ASSESSMENT OF TARGET WORDS

Learning a word is a gradual process.

- First, you learn to *recognize* the word. This means you know something about its spelling, pronunciation, and meanings.
- Next, you learn to *use* the word. This requires that you understand its spelling, pronunciation, grammar, and much more.

When you truly know a word, you can both recognize it and use it accurately.

Think carefully about how well you know each target word in this unit. They are listed in the objectives box, above. Then, write each word in the appropriate column in this chart.

I have never seen the word before.	I have seen the word but am not sure what it means.	I understand the word when I see or hear it in a sentence.	I have tried to use this word, but I am not sure I am using it correctly.	I use the word with confidence in either speaking *or* writing.	I use the word with confidence, both in speaking *and* writing.

BEFORE YOU READ

Read these questions. Discuss your answers in a small group.

1. Do you know how to ride a bicycle? Who taught you to ride? What was the hardest thing to learn?
2. What are some reasons that people ride bicycles?
3. If you could change or improve bicycles, what would you want to do?

READING STRATEGY: Previewing

> Most good readers spend a few minutes *previewing* before they begin to read. Previewing a book or article means looking it over to get a general idea of what it will be about. It allows you to recall what you already know about a topic, and what you would like to learn.

Preview Reading 1, below, by answering these questions. Discuss your answers with a partner.

1. Read the summary printed above the article. In a few words, it tells what the article will be about. What do you expect to learn about in the article?
2. Look at the pictures and captions. What information do they give you about the topic that words cannot describe?
3. Read the title. You already know that the article will be about old bicycles, but what does the word "history" suggest? What kind of information *might* be in the article? Put a check (✓) next those items.

.... when the bicycle was invented   .... how to use bicycles for exercise

.... a description of the first bicycle   .... who invented the bicycle

.... changes in the bicycle over time   .... how people reacted to the invention

.... famous bicycle races   .... how bicycle tires are made

READ

This article tells about the many changes in bicycles during the past 200 years.

The History of Bicycles

The bicycle was not invented by one individual or in one country. It took nearly 100 years and many **individuals** for the modern bicycle to be born. By the end of those 100
5 years, bicycles had **revolutionized** the way people traveled from place to place.

Bicycles first appeared in Scotland in the early 1800s, and were called velocipedes. These early bicycles had two wheels, but they had no pedals.
10 The rider sat on a pillow and walked his feet along the ground to move his velocipede forward.

Soon a French inventor added pedals to the front wheel. Instead of walking their vehicles, riders used their feet to turn the pedals.
15 However, pedaling was hard because velocipedes

were very heavy. The **framework** was made of solid steel tubes and the wooden wheels were covered with steel. Even so, velocipedes were popular among rich young men, who raced them in Paris parks.

Because velocipedes were so hard to ride, no one thought about using them for transportation. People didn't ride velocipedes to the market or to their **jobs**. Instead, people thought velocipedes were just toys.

Around 1870, American manufacturers saw that velocipedes were very popular **overseas**. They began building velocipedes, too, but with one difference. They made the frameworks from hollow steel tubes. This **alteration** made velocipedes much lighter, but riders still had to work hard to pedal just a short distance. In addition, roads were bumpy so steering was difficult. In fact, most riders preferred indoor tracks where they could rent a velocipede for a small **fee** and take riding lessons.

Subsequent changes by British engineers altered the wheels to make pedaling more efficient. They saw that when a rider turned the pedals once, the front wheel turned once. If the front wheel was small, the bicycle traveled just a small distance with each turn. They reasoned that if the front wheel were larger, the bicycle would travel a greater distance. So they **designed** a bicycle with a giant front wheel. They made the rear wheel small. Its **primary** purpose was to help the rider balance. Balancing was hard

The high-wheeler made pedaling more efficient.

---
[1] *axle*: the center bar of a wheel

because the rider had to sit high above the giant front wheel in order to reach the pedals. This meant he was in danger of falling off the bicycle and **injuring** himself if he lost his balance. Despite this **inherent** danger, "high wheelers" became very popular in England.

American manufacturers once again tried to design a better bicycle. Their goal was to make a safer bicycle. They **substituted** a small wheel for the giant front wheel and put the driving mechanism in a larger rear wheel. It would be impossible for a rider to pedal the rear wheel, so engineers designed a system of foot levers. By pressing first the right one and then the left, the rider moved a long metal bar up and down. This bar turned the rear axle[1]. This axle turned the rear wheel and the bicycle moved forward. Because the new safety bicycle **minimized** the dangers inherent in bicycle riding, more and more people began using bicycles in their daily activities.

Levers replace pedals, for a little while.

The British altered the design one last time. They made the two wheels equal in size and created a mechanism that uses a chain to turn the rear wheel. With this final change, the modern bicycle was born.

Subsequent improvements, such as brakes, rubber tires, and lights were added to make bicycles more comfortable to ride. By 1900, bicycle riding had become very popular with men and women of all ages. Bicycles revolutionized the way people traveled. Today, millions of people worldwide ride bicycles for transportation, enjoyment, sport, and exercise.

READING COMPREHENSION

Mark each statement as *T* (True) or *F* (False) according to the information in Reading 1. Use your dictionary to check the meaning of new words.

.... 1. Many individuals took part in creating the modern bicycle.

.... 2. The first bicycle revolutionized travel in Scotland and overseas.

.... 3. Early velocipedes had frameworks made of solid steel tubes.

.... 4. American manufacturers substituted hollow steel tubes for the solid tubes.

.... 5. People in Paris paid a fee to ride velocipedes to their jobs.

.... 6. The primary purpose of the giant front wheel was to help the rider balance.

.... 7. American manufacturers designed a bicycle with a small rear wheel that was inherently safer.

.... 8. The modern bicycle was born when British engineers subsequently altered the wheels again and made them equal in size.

STEP I VOCABULARY ACTIVITIES: Word Level

A. Read this passage about the Tour de France, a world-famous bicycle race. In each sentence, circle the one word or phrase in parentheses ( ) that has the same meaning as the underlined word in the sentence. Compare your answers with a partner.

1. The course for the Tour de France is <u>altered</u> (*measured* / *changed* / *marked*) every year, but it is always about 4,000 kilometers, or 2,500 miles.

2. The course is <u>designed</u> (*located* / *expected* / *planned*) to travel through towns, up steep mountains, and across flat lands.

3. Riders come from all over Europe as well as from <u>overseas</u> (*islands* / *other continents* / *oceans*) to take part in the 22-day race.

4. The race is divided into 20 stages, or parts. The rider who wins one stage has the honor of wearing a yellow Tour shirt in the <u>subsequent</u> (*final* / *longest* / *next*) stage.

5. The rider who has the fastest race time in all of the stages is the overall winner. Lance Armstrong is the only <u>individual</u> (*person* / *man* / *foreigner*) to win seven Tour de France competitions.

6. The <u>framework</u> (*mechanism* / *structure* / *wheel*) of modern racing bicycles is made of lightweight steel, aluminum, titanium, and carbon fiber tubes.

7. The recent use of lightweight frameworks brought about <u>revolutionary</u> (*unwanted* / *unfair* / *great*) changes in the 100-year-old race.

8. Teams pay an entrance <u>fee</u> (*payment* / *tax* / *salary*) to join the Tour de France. The fees create the prize money paid to the winning teams.

9. Riders must be good athletes to meet the physical demands that are an <u>inherent</u> (*unexpected* / *natural* / *dangerous*) part of a long race.

10. If a rider is <u>injured</u> (*sick / bleeding / hurt*), he tries to <u>minimize</u> (*lessen / hide / endure*) the pain so he can stay in the race.

11. If the pain is too bad, the coach can assign a teammate to <u>substitute for</u> (*help / take out / replace*) the injured rider.

12. The <u>primary</u> (*main / total / easiest*) <u>job</u> (*purpose / employment / task*) of a Tour coach is to help his team win.

B. Think about the problems that racing cyclists can have. Match the problem on the right with the item that can minimize it on the left. Then, tell a partner how the two ideas are connected.

...*a*... **1.** knee braces   **a.** stress on knees

        Knee braces can minimize stress on knees.

.... **2.** low handle bars   **b.** thirst

.... **3.** a helmet   **c.** sunburn

.... **4.** long sleeves   **d.** sprains

.... **5.** water   **e.** head injuries

.... **6.** ice   **f.** air drag

The adjective *inherent* refers to a natural, built-in quality of a person, object, or activity. *Inherently* is the adverb form.

    *Riders are aware of the **inherent** danger of bicycle racing.*

    *Bicycle racing is **inherently** dangerous.*

C. Which of these sports do you think are inherently dangerous? Put a check (✓) next to them. Add one more. Then, discuss the reasons for your choices in a small group.

.... snow skiing   .... race-car driving

.... boxing   .... horseback riding

.... soccer   .... motorcycle racing

.... basketball   .... swimming

.... long-distance running   .... mountain climbing

.... tennis   .... Other: ....

Primary refers to something that is first, main, or basic. Here are some examples of collocations (words that go together) using the word *primary*:

primary colors	primary elections
primary school	primary care physician

D. Match the worker on the left with his or her primary job on the right. Then, with a partner, discuss the answers to the questions below.

.... **1.** taxi driver

.... **2.** architect

.... **3.** tailor

.... **4.** international airline pilot

.... **5.** doctor

.... **6.** substitute teacher

.... **7.** janitor

a. altering clothing to fit individuals

b. teaching the classes of a teacher who is absent

c. driving people from place to place for a fee

d. designing buildings

e. cleaning and taking care of buildings

f. helping individuals who are injured or sick

g. flying airplanes overseas

Which of the workers in activity D must do their jobs primarily during the day? Which of them might also work primarily at night?

STEP II VOCABULARY ACTIVITIES: Sentence Level

Word Form Chart			
Noun	Verb	Adjective	Adverb
revolution	revolutionize	revolutionary	....

The central meaning of *revolution* is "turning" or "changing." It can refer to one thing rotating around a central point, like the Earth's revolution around the sun. It can also mean "changing or trying to change the political system by violent action."

In this unit, *revolution* is used to mean "a complete change in methods, opinions, etc., often as a result of progress."

Bicycles led to a **revolution** *in transportation.*

Bicycles **revolutionized** *the way people traveled from place to place.*

Bicycles were a **revolutionary** *idea.*

E. Rewrite these sentences two ways. Use a different form of *revolution* in each sentence.

1. The addition of sound changed the way motion pictures told stories. (noun, verb)

   The sound revolution changed the way motion pictures told stories. (noun)
   The addition of sound revolutionized the way motion pictures told a story. (verb)

2. The jet engine caused a change in air travel. (verb, adj.)

....

....

3. Alfred Nobel created a new substance that he called "dynamite." (noun, adj.)

....

....

4. The discovery of x-rays changed medical science. (noun, adj.)

....

....

F. Make new words related to bicycles by substituting one or two letters in these words. Tell a partner how you made the new words.

1. like: .... *Substitute a B for the L to make the word bike.* ....

2. chair: ....

3. steel: ....

4. sent: ....

5. time: ....

6. broke: ....

7. hide: ....

8. petal: ....

Subsequent is an adjective that refers to something that is later than or follows something else. The adverb form is *subsequently*.

*Henry Ford's first car was called the Model T. A **subsequent** car was called the Model A.*

*Henry Ford created the Model T in 1908. **Subsequently**, he built the Model A.*

G. Complete each sentence with *subsequent* AND *substitute*. Be sure to use the correct form of each word.

1. The wheels of the first velocipedes had no pedals, but a French inventor .... wheels that had pedals.

2. European velocipedes were heavy because the framework was made of solid steel tubes. The .... of hollow steel tubes by American manufacturers made the vehicles much lighter.

3. The high wheeler had a small rear wheel. A .... change by American manufacturers .... the larger rear wheel for the smaller one.

BEFORE YOU READ

Read these questions. Discuss your answers in a small group.

1. How much do you walk in your daily activities? Do you sometimes wish you could walk faster? When?
2. How do you decide if you should walk, ride a bicycle, or drive when you go somewhere?
3. Have you ever seen a Segway? Describe where you saw it and what it looked like.

READING STRATEGY

Preview Reading 2 by answering these questions. Discuss your answers with a partner.

1. Look at the title of the article. Does the title tell you what it will be about? What does the word "future" in the title suggest about the article? How do you think this article will be different from the previous reading in this unit?
2. Look at the picture in the article. Does it help explain what a Segway is?
3. What questions *might* be answered in the article? Put a check (✓) next to them.

.... Where are Segways used now?   .... Where is the engine?

.... Who will ride Segways?   .... What color are they?

.... Who invented the Segway?   .... What are they used for?

.... When was the Segway invented?   .... How many Segways are in Paris?

READ

This newspaper article poses questions about the future of personal transport.

Segway into the Future

Will the electric vehicle known as *the Segway* alter the ways that individuals get around? Dean Kamer, the inventor of the Segway, believes that this revolutionary vehicle will someday
5 substitute for the bicycles and automobiles that now crowd our cities. When he introduced the Segway in 2001, he believed it would change our lives.

Although the Segway uses up-to-the-minute
10 technology, it looks very ordinary. The metal framework of the Segway consists of a platform where an individual stands. Attached to the front of the platform is a tall post with handles for the driver to hold. On each side of the
15 platform is a wide, rubber wheel. Except for these two wheels, there are no mechanical parts on the Segway. It has no engine, no brakes, no pedal power, no gears, and no steering wheel.
20 Instead it uses a computer system that imitates the ability of humans to keep their balance.

This system seems
25 to move the Segway in response to the driver's

thoughts. For example, when the driver thinks, "Go forward," the Segway moves forward, and when the driver thinks, "Stop," it stops. The Segway is not really responding to the driver's thoughts, but to the tiny changes in balance that the driver makes as he prepares his body to move forward or to stop. For example, when the driver thinks about moving forward, he actually leans slightly forward, and when he thinks of stopping or slowing, the driver leans slightly back.

The computer system checks the driver's body movements about 100 times every second and instantly moves the Segway accordingly. If the driver leans forward, the Segway moves forward. If the driver leans back, the Segway slows down. If the driver continues to lean back, the Segway stops. If the driver leans to the right or left, the Segway turns in response.

The Segway is powered by batteries that allow it to travel about 17 miles on one battery charge. It is designed for short-range, low-speed operation. It has three speed settings. The slowest is the setting for learning, with speeds of up to 6 miles per hour. Next is the sidewalk setting, with speeds of up to 9 miles per hour. The highest setting allows the driver to travel up to 12.5 miles per hour in open, flat areas. At all three speed settings, the Segway can go wherever a person can walk, both indoors and outdoors.

Workers who must walk a lot in their jobs might be the primary users of Segways. For example, police officers could drive Segways to patrol city streets, and mail carriers could drive from house to house to deliver letters and packages. Farmers could quickly inspect distant fields and barns, and rangers could more easily patrol forests, beaches, or parks. Security guards could protect neighborhoods or large buildings.

Any task requiring a lot of walking could be made easier. In cities, shoppers could leave their cars at home and ride Segways from store to store. Also, people who cannot comfortably walk due to age, illness, or injury could minimize their walking but still be able to go many places on a Segway.

Why is it, then, that our job sites, parks, and shopping centers have not been subsequently filled with Segways since they were introduced in 2001? Why hasn't the expected revolution taken place? Studies have shown that Segways can help workers get more done in a shorter time. This saves money. Engineers admire Segways as a technological marvel.

Businesses, government agencies, and individuals, however, have been unwilling to accept the Segway. Yes, there have been some successes. In a few cities, for example, mail carriers drive Segways on their routes, and police officers patrol on Segways. San Francisco, California, and Florence, Italy, are among several cities in the world that offer tours on Segways for a small fee. Occasionally you will see golfers riding Segways around golf courses. Throughout the world more than 150 security agencies use Segways, and China has recently entered the overseas market. These examples are encouraging, but can hardly be called a revolution.

The primary reason seems to be that people have an inherent fear of doing something new. They fear others will laugh at them for buying a "toy." They fear losing control of the vehicle. They fear being injured. They fear not knowing the rules for using a Segway. They fear making people angry if they ride on the sidewalk. All these fears and others have kept sales low.

The inventor explained why people have been slow to accept the Segway. He said, "We didn't realize that although technology moves very quickly, people's mind-set changes very slowly." Perhaps a hundred years from now millions of people around the world will be riding Segways.

READING COMPREHENSION

Mark each statement as *T* (True) or *F* (False) according to the information in Reading 2. Use your dictionary to check the meaning of new words.

.... **1.** The Segway's framework consists of a platform and a post with handles.

.... **2.** The driver can alter the direction of the Segway by leaning to the left or right.

.... **3.** The Segway was primarily designed for people who cannot walk comfortably.

.... **4.** Workers have been injured while riding Segways on their jobs.

.... **5.** If the driver leans forward, the Segway subsequently slows down.

.... **6.** People seem to have an inherent fear of electric vehicles.

.... **7.** For a fee, people can take a tour on a Segway in some cities.

.... **8.** Segways are being used in the U.S. as well as overseas.

STEP I VOCABULARY ACTIVITIES: Word Level

A. Use the target vocabulary in the box to complete this story. The words in parentheses can help you.

alter	injured	primary
designed	had a job	revolutionized
framework	an inherent	subsequent
individual	minimize	substituted

In 1901, Glenn Curtiss was 23 years old and .... manufacturing
                                                         (1. *worked at*)
and selling bicycles. He had .... love of speed. He wanted to find a
                                    (2. *a natural*)
way to .... bicycles so they could go faster than a rider could pedal
        (3. *change*)
them. Glenn .... an engine that .... a tomato
              (4. *made the plans for*)   (5. *replaced*)
can for a carburetor. He attached the engine to the drive mechanism of a bicycle.

However, the engine did not make the bicycle go much faster despite the loud noise

it made. A .... engine that Glenn built was too heavy and the bicycle
            (6. *later*)
was hard to balance. Riders often tipped over and .... themselves.
                                                       (7. *hurt*)
The heavy weight of the engine was the .... problem he had to solve.
                                           (8. *main*)
After many tries to .... the weight, he solved the problem by making
                     (9. *lessen*)
the .... stronger. He began racing his "motorcycle." In 1907, Glenn
     (10. *structure*)
set a speed record. He went 136 miles per hour, faster than any .... in
                                                                    (11. *person*)
the world had ever traveled. Glenn's invention .... bicycle riding.
                                                   (12. *created a big change in*)

A word analogy shows the relationship between two sets of words. To solve an analogy, you must identify how the words in the first set are related. Here are some examples.

apple : fruit	example	An *apple* is an example of a *fruit*.
pretty : lovely	synonym	*Pretty* and *lovely* have similar meanings.
young : old	antonym	*Young* and *old* have opposite meanings.
bicycle : ride	action	*Ride* is the action when you use a *bicycle*.
room : house	part	A *room* is part of a *house*.

To finish an analogy, think of a word to complete the second set of words that has the same relationship as the first set.

apple : fruit AS carrot : ....

An apple is an example of a fruit, so the missing word is *vegetable*. *Carrot* is an example of a *vegetable*.

You say an analogy like this: "*Apple* is to *fruit* as *carrot* is to *vegetable*."

B. Use the target vocabulary in the box to complete these analogies. Then write the type of relationship each analogy has. Compare answers with a partner.

fee	job	primary
individual	minimize	subsequently
injury	overseas	

Relationship

1. bouquet : flower AS crowd : ....*individual*........   ....*part*........

2. car : damage AS person : ....

3. save : spend AS increase : ....

4. nation : country AS abroad : ....

5. write : check AS pay : ....

6. false : true AS last : ....

7. bus : vehicle AS bus driver : ....

8. before : after AS earlier : ....

A *framework* is a structure upon which other parts are built or attached. On a bicycle, the wheels, pedals, and handlebars are attached to the steel framework. Sometimes, *framework* refers to the basis or foundation of something.

*The **frameworks** of early velocipedes were made of solid steel tubes.*

*A good education forms the **framework** for a successful career.*

C. Match the frameworks on the right with the object or system that they support on the left. Then, tell a partner how the two ideas are connected.

.... **1.** the human body   **a.** steel beams

.... **2.** many governments   **b.** an interesting plot

.... **3.** a skyscraper   **c.** the number 10

.... **4.** the metric system   **d.** a constitution

.... **5.** a good book   **e.** the skeleton

To *alter* something means "to make something different in some way, but without changing it completely." If you alter something, you have made an *alteration*.

Not everything can be altered. Some things are *unalterable*: they are not able to be altered. Many things, however, are *alterable*: they can be altered.

D. Work with a partner. Imagine that you have borrowed a friend's bicycle for the weekend. Which things can you alter? Which things cannot be altered on a borrowed bicycle? Write *A* for each item that is alterable. Write *U* for each item that is unalterable.

.... the speed of the bicycle   .... the size of the wheels

.... the color of the framework   .... the direction the bicycle turns

.... the height of the seat   .... the speed that the wheels turn

.... the design of the bicycle   .... the mirrors on the handlebars

STEP II VOCABULARY ACTIVITIES: Sentence Level

Word Form Chart			
Noun	Verb	Adjective	Adverb
design designer	design	designed	....
individual individuality	individualize	individual individualized	individually

E. Pinewood Derby is a car race sponsored by the Boy Scouts of America. The cars are small—just seven inches long. Rewrite these sentences about the Pinewood Derby to include the word in parentheses. Discuss your sentences with a partner.

1. Each boy works by himself to make his own cars. (*individually*)

2. First each boy makes a plan of his car on paper. (*design*, verb)

3. He wants to make his car look like no other cars in the derby, so it will be special. (*individualize*)

4. He can show his unique personality in many ways. Some boys plan their cars to look like a snake or a hot dog, for example. (*individuality*, *design*)

5. To build the car, the creator traces his plan on a block of wood and carves out the shape. Then he attaches the wheels and paints his car. (*designer*, *design*)

6. On the day of the race, the Boy Scouts roll their cars down a sloped board one at a time. The fastest car down the board wins a prize. (*individually*).

7. The judges give separate prizes for the funniest car, the scariest car, and other categories. (*individual*, adj.)

8. Every car is a winner. The contest is planned to show every boy's special qualities. (*designed*, verb; *individuality*)

F. The bicycle and the Segway are very different kinds of vehicles. Write one sentence about velocipedes or bicycles and another sentence about Segways using the word given. You may use different forms of the word (for example, *revolutionary* or *revolutionize*).

1. revolution

   ....

   ....

2. designer

   ....

   ....

3. power

   ....

   ....

4. balance

   ....

   ....

5. popular

   ....

   ....

G. In your notebook, write three sentences that might have been included in an 1885 advertisement to sell high wheeler bicycles. Next write three sentences that might be included in a 2010 advertisement to sell Segways. Be prepared to present your work in class.

H. Self-Assessment Review: Go back to page 1 and reassess your knowledge of the target vocabulary. How has your understanding of the words changed? What words do you feel most comfortable with now?

WRITING AND DISCUSSION TOPICS

1. Look up the word *segue* in a dictionary. How is it pronounced? What does it mean? Why do you think Dean Kamer named his invention "Segway"?

2. People have been slow to accept the Segway. Make a list of ideas that Dean Kamer might use to encourage people to ride Segways.

3. Imagine that you work as a police officer in a small city. Your department has purchased a Segway for each officer who patrols the city streets. Yesterday was your first day patrolling on your Segway. Use your imagination and write a story about how you used the Segway, what you liked, and what problems you had.

4. Reading 1 ends with, "Today, millions of people worldwide ride bicycles for transportation, enjoyment, sport, and exercise." Describe examples of each of these uses.

5. The Segway was not designed to be used for sport; however, some people believe that certain team sports could be adapted for players riding Segways. What sports could be adapted to use Segways? How would the players use them?

6. Dean Kamen said, ". . . although technology moves very quickly, people's mind-set changes very slowly." Do you agree with this statement? Can you think of other inventions besides the Segway that this applies to? Can you think of some inventions that people accepted very quickly?

FIGHTING DISEASES

In this unit, you will

- read about the causes and effects of malaria in sub-Saharan Africa.
- read about sources of new medicines.
- practice finding main ideas in your reading.
- increase your understanding of the target academic words for this unit:

access	cooperate	intense	ministry	priority
accompany	decline	labor	occur	reside
conflict	implement	medical	practitioner	

SELF-ASSESSMENT OF TARGET WORDS

Think carefully about how well you know each target word in this unit. Then, write it in the appropriate column in the chart.

I have never seen the word before.	I have seen the word but am not sure what it means.	I understand the word when I see or hear it in a sentence.	I have tried to use this word, but I am not sure I am using it correctly.	I use the word with confidence in either speaking *or* writing.	I use the word with confidence, both in speaking *and* writing.

MORE WORDS YOU'LL NEED

infect: to cause someone to have a disease or illness

resistant: not harmed by something

parasite: a plant or animal that lives in or on another plant or animal and gets its food from it

prevent: to stop something from occurring

BEFORE YOU READ

Read these questions. Discuss your answers in a small group.

1. Have you ever been very sick? What did you do to get well? How long did it take you to get well?

2. What are some ways to prevent an illness?

3. Do you know of any insects that are helpful to humans? How do they help? Do you know of any insects that are harmful to humans? How are they harmful?

READ

This article includes information from the Centers for Disease Control and Prevention (CDC), the principal public health agency in the United States. It was founded in 1946 to help control malaria. Today, the CDC leads public health efforts to prevent and control infectious diseases.

The Battle Against Malaria

Malaria is a serious health problem. It is a leading cause of death in many countries. It **occurs** mostly in tropical and subtropical parts of the world, including parts of Africa,
5 Asia, South America, Central America, and the Middle East. The place most intensely affected by malaria is Africa south of the Sahara Desert. About 60% of the world's malaria cases and 80% of malaria deaths occur there. Even though
10 the causes of malaria in this region are well understood, international health agencies are finding that controlling it is still an enormous and difficult task.

Because malaria is passed from mosquitoes to
15 people and from people to mosquitoes, we can think of the disease as a cycle[1]. The malaria cycle begins with tiny parasites that **reside** in the bodies of *Anopheles* mosquitoes. These deadly parasites cause malaria. When a female mosquito
20 bites a human, the mosquito draws off blood. It also leaves malaria parasites in the human's skin. These parasites quickly multiply inside the human and cause the individual to feel sick.

If a mosquito bites a human who is sick with
25 malaria, parasites from the human enter the body of the mosquito. When that mosquito bites another human, it will leave parasites in the other human's skin. In the malaria cycle, humans get parasites from mosquitoes and they
30 also give parasites to mosquitoes.

Becoming infected with malaria is a medical emergency. The first symptoms of malaria are fever, chills, sweating, **intense** headache, and muscle pains. Nausea and vomiting often
35 **accompany** these symptoms. Immediate **medical** treatment must be a **priority** for people who are infected. They must take medicines that will kill the parasites. If medical treatment is started soon enough, sick
40 individuals can be cured. If they do not, malaria can cause serious illness or even death.

Breaking the malaria cycle in Africa

---

[1] *cycle*: a series of events that always recur in the same order

Malaria in tropical Africa could be controlled in two ways. First, it could be controlled by killing the parasites that cause the illness. If every infected person quickly took malaria medicine, most would be well in a few days. Mosquitoes could not get malaria parasites from healthy individuals, so malaria would not spread. Unfortunately, many people live in far-away villages without **access** to quick medical care. Another problem is that the ability of quinine (the primary medicine used against malaria) to kill parasites has **declined** over time. There is hope, however, for a new drug combination, called ACT. It is being used successfully to treat people who have malaria.

Malaria could also be controlled by stopping the mosquitoes. One way would be to get rid of the pools of water where they lay their eggs. Also, insecticide[2] could be sprayed in wet areas and around buildings to kill mosquitoes. Finally, people could be told to sleep under bed nets to prevent mosquitoes from biting them at night. Bed nets sprayed with insecticide would both stop and kill mosquitoes.

---

[2] *insecticide*: a poison that kills insects

It is very difficult, however, to **implement** these plans. People in this region are poor—and made poorer by malaria because they may be too weak to work. They cannot afford to pay for medical care or to buy bed nets. If they are not educated, the people may be unwilling to **cooperate** with government efforts to help them. Their old beliefs about illness may **conflict** with modern attempts to cure or prevent malaria.

There are other problems, too. Health **ministries** do not have the money to build clinics or hire trained medical **practitioners**. They do not have the money to buy insecticide and pay a **labor** force to spray regularly. And the frequent rainfall would make it impossible to get rid of pools of water where mosquitoes lay eggs.

Helping African nations control malaria is now a top priority of many relief organizations. The World Health Organization and Doctors Without Borders are just two of many organizations offering help—and hope—to the people of sub-Saharan Africa.

READING COMPREHENSION

Mark each statement as *T* (True) or *F* (False) according to the information in Reading 1. Use your dictionary to check the meaning of new words.

__T__ 1. Malaria occurs mostly in tropical and subtropical parts of the world.

__T__ 2. Deadly malaria parasites reside in the bodies of mosquitoes.

__F__ 3. Intense coughing and sneezing often accompany the fever of malaria.

__T__ 4. Old beliefs may conflict with modern ways to cure or prevent illness.

__T__ 5. Getting fast medical attention after becoming ill is a priority.

__T__ 6. Sleeping under bed nets would lead to a decline in malaria.

__T__ 7. Health ministries in poor countries often cannot afford to implement plans to control malaria.

__F__ 8. Most people in tropical Africa have easy access to medical practitioners.

__F__ 9. Educated people are not willing to cooperate with government plans to help them.

__T__ 10. A large labor force would be needed to spray insecticide regularly.

READING STRATEGY: Finding the Main Idea

The *topic* of an article refers to what the article is about. The *main idea* of an article goes one step further. The main idea includes the topic and also what the writer wants to say about the topic. For example,

Topic	Main idea
vegetables	*several reasons why kids hate vegetables*

The main idea of an article is often clearly stated in the first paragraph, usually in the first or last sentence. It can also be stated in the second paragraph or in the last paragraph, which often summarizes the article. The main idea may be a full sentence or just a few words.

Each paragraph in an article contributes its own facts, definitions, and examples that help explain the main idea of the article. This means that each paragrah has its own main idea, which is often in the first sentence of the paragraph.

A. Reread the first paragraph of Reading 1. Find the sentence that tells you the *main idea*—what the writer wants to say about malaria—and circle it. Then, write the most important part of the sentence here, as the main idea.

....

....

B. Reread paragraph 2 and find the sentence that states the main idea. What is the main idea? Circle your answer here.

  a. The beginning of the malaria cycle

  b. *Anapheles* mosquitos

  c. Parasites in the human's skin

C. Reread paragraph 4 and find the sentence that states the main idea. What is the main idea? Circle your answer here.

  a. Malaria can cause death

  b. Becoming infected is a medical emergency

  c. Sick people must take medicine

D. Reread paragraph 7 and find the sentence that states the main idea. What is the main idea? Circle your answer here.

  a. The people of the region need education about malaria

  b. Plans to prevent malaria are difficult to implement

  c. Malaria makes people more poor because they cannot work

STEP I VOCABULARY ACTIVITIES: Word Level

A. A *practitioner* is a formal word to describe someone who practices a specific profession. Match these practitioners with their descriptions. Compare answers with a partner.

.... **1.** a practitioner of law

.... **2.** a nurse-practitioner

.... **3.** a practitioner of sports

.... **4.** a practitioner of education

a. a nurse who has had extra training and can perform some services of a doctor

b. someone who teaches others

c. someone licensed to represent someone else in legal matters

d. an athlete

A *ministry* is a governmental department that oversees the administration of one area of responsibility. A ministry is headed by a *minister*. He or she is in charge of the *ministerial* duties of the department. The head of a government is often called the *prime minister*.

Not all countries use these titles, however. The United States government, for example, has *departments* headed by *secretaries*. The head of the government is called the *president*.

Note: Another common use of the word *minister* is for a church leader, usually in a Christian church. The *ministry* is his or her profession. He or she *ministers* to the people in the church.

B. Match each government ministry to its area of responsibility. Then, tell a partner how the two ideas are connected.

.... **1.** Health Ministry

.... **2.** Finance Ministry

.... **3.** Labor Ministry

.... **4.** Agricultural Ministry

.... **5.** Transportation Ministry

a. the national budget

b. working conditions in factories

c. airlines and trains

d. hospitals and healthcare practitioners

e. farm products

Now, tell a partner the title of the person in charge of each ministry.

> The **Minister** of Health heads the Health **Ministry**.

C. Which of these things should be treated medically? Put a check (✓) next to them. Why do you think they require medical attention? Discuss your ideas with a partner.

.... **1.** a broken arm

.... **2.** hair loss

.... **3.** a broken fingernail

.... **4.** an earache

.... **5.** a heart attack

.... **6.** a high fever

A *conflict* (noun, pronounced CON-flict) is a disagreement or a difference in ideas or plans. It can be serious or not, depending on the context.

Two nations had an armed **conflict** *that lasted five years.*

Ms. Ellis had a schedule **conflict**. *She had two meetings at 9 a.m.*

To *conflict* (verb, pronounced con-FLICT) means "to happen at the same time" or "to be in disagreement." The adjective form is *conflicting*.

Her staff meeting **conflicts** *with a sales meeting.*

Two professors had **conflicting** *ideas about history.*

D. Which of these pairs of newspaper hcadlines have conflicting information? Discuss with a partner why they conflict or don't conflict.

1. **a.** HEALTH MINISTRY REPORTS A DECLINE IN MALARIA
   b. MALARIA NUMBERS INCREASE THIS YEAR

2. **a.** GOVERNMENT IMPLEMENTS NEW HEALTH PROGRAM
   b. NEW HEALTH PROGRAM PUT INTO SERVICE

3. **a.** STAFF TO ACCOMPANY PRIME MINISTER ON OVERSEAS TRIP
   b. PRIME MINISTER TO GO OVERSEAS ALONE

E. *Labor* **refers to hard or difficult work. What might these people be doing when they are laboring? Which people are probably paid for their labor? Which ones probably receive no money for their labor? Discuss your ideas with a partner.**

1. a student
2. a farmer
3. an auto mechanic
4. a cook
5. a housewife
6. a poet
7. a musician
8. a gardener

STEP II VOCABULARY ACTIVITIES: Sentence Level

Word Form Chart			
Noun	Verb	Adjective	Adverb
intensity intensification	intensify	intense intensive	intensely intensively

F. Read this information about a common public health problem in primary schools. In your notebook, restate the sentences, including a form of *intense*.

1. Head lice, tiny insects that lay their eggs in the hair of humans, have been a serious problem in primary schools for many years.

    Head lice have been an intense problem in primary schools for many years.

2. Young children share combs, hats, and other headgear, which increases the chance that they may pick up head lice from a friend.

3. Parents are sometimes extremely embarrassed when the school informs them that their child has head lice, but it is not their fault.

4. There is enormous conflict in some schools about whether children should be allowed to attend school when they have head lice.

5. The conflict increases when some parents send their children to school with head lice, but others keep their child at home when a classmate has lice.

6. The only symptom of head lice is very strong itching of the head.

7. Getting rid of lice requires a lot of hard work.

8. The child's hair must be washed with a strong chemical rinse. The parent must then closely search for remaining lice eggs and pick them out.

The *priority* of something refers its importance or value in relation to other things. It is usually accompanied by an adjective.

  *My children are my <u>highest</u> **priority** in life.*

  *Hospitals give patients with minor injuries the <u>lowest</u> **priority**.*

When no adjective accompanies the word, it means simply *important* or *not important*.

  *Time is a **priority** here.*   In this situation, time is important.

  *Color is not a **priority**.*   Color is not important in this situation.

G. Imagine that you work with the organization Doctors Without Borders. Your team has just arrived in a country where most of the people are sick with malaria. With a partner, prioritize these actions—rank them for importance. Write *1* for highest priority, *2* for the next highest, etc. Give reasons for your prioritization.

.... spraying homes with insecticide

.... cutting down tall grass

.... giving medicine to sick people

.... giving food to sick people

.... getting rid of pools of water

.... teaching people to wash their hands

Word Form Chart			
Noun	Verb	Adjective	Adverb
resident residence residents residences (people) (places)	reside	residential	residentially

H. In your notebook, rewrite this memo to include the words *priority*, *intense*, and *reside*. Try to use other target words from this unit also. Be prepared to present your work in class.

> To: The Village Rescue Team
> From: Relief camp director
> Re: People living in villages affected by the yesterday's earthquake
>
> The earthquake yesterday morning injured many people who live in nearby villages. The strong vibrations also destroyed many homes.
>
> The first thing we have to do is to take care of the injured people. Next, we need to set up tents where people can live until their homes are rebuilt. There is plenty to eat here, so finding more food is not so important right now.
>
> I have asked the village leader to decide which village services should be restored and in what order. His list will help us plan our schedule.
>
> As more people come to the relief camp, our work will probably get more difficult. Help each other and try to make the best of this very difficult time.

READING 2

BEFORE YOU READ

Discuss the answers to these questions in a small group.

1. What medicines do you take when you are sick? How well do they work?

2. Did your parents or grandparents have some old-fashioned ways to treat illnesses? Did those treatments work?

3. What advertisements have you seen for medicines on TV or in magazines? What kind of promises do they make?

This article from a popular science magazine describes some of the sources for new medicines.

Searching for New Medicines

Over time, new diseases develop that cannot be cured with the medicines we have. Also, many medicines that once cured common diseases sometimes lose their power to cure. For these reasons, modern drug companies are constantly looking for new medicines to help doctors cure both new and common diseases. One place that drug companies are looking is in the rainforests of the world. Scientists believe that new plants from the rainforests or simple medicines from rainforest peoples might be sources for future miracle drugs.

Four hundred years ago, just such a miracle drug was found to cure malaria. In 1633, a fortunate event occurred. A Spanish priest was sent as a missionary to Peru. He wanted to minister to the native Indians there and convert them to his religion. While he was teaching, however, he learned something. The village healer—the only medical practitioner the people had ever known—was making a powder from the bark[1] of the cinchona tree. He used this powder to cure malaria. The priest brought some of this miracle powder home to Europe, where malaria was a serious disease at the time. Europeans began using the bark to cure malaria. Soon Europeans implemented overseas searches for sources of the tree bark. After many years, scientists identified the ingredient in the tree bark that cured malaria. It was quinine. By 1827, quinine was commercially produced and became the primary treatment for malaria throughout the world. By the 1960s, however, quinine's ability to kill the malaria parasite had declined because the parasite was becoming resistant to it.

About this time, another fortunate event occurred. Scientists in China were digging up ancient cities. One city was a place where people had resided 2,000 years earlier. The

Early missionaries learned from native healers.

scientists discovered that the ancient people had used a plant, called wormwood, to cure fevers. Scientists collected living samples of the plant to test. They found that wormwood contained *artemisinin*. This chemical killed malaria parasites. Today, artemisinin is used in various mixtures with other drugs (Artemisinin Combination Therapy, or ACT) to treat people who have malaria.

Aspirin is another ancient medicine. Its history dates back over 2,000 years, when ancient Greek physicians made a tea from willow bark to ease pain and lower fever. People continued to use willow bark as a home remedy for centuries. Modern scientists identified *salicylic acid* as the special ingredient in the bark that eased pain and fever. Soon, drug companies were making aspirin tablets containing salicylic acid. Today, aspirin is one of the most widely used drugs in the world. Around 100 billion aspirin tablets are produced each year.

Not all medical histories are centuries old. The story of *taxol* is an example of how miracle drugs are still being found in the world's forests. In 1966, scientists discovered a powerful chemical in the bark of the Pacific yew tree. This chemical could stop cell growth. They believed it would be useful in treating the unnatural cell growth of cancer. Soon, taxol was being used in intensive treatments for certain kinds of cancer.

---

[1] *bark*: the hard outer covering of a tree

70　Scientists think that many medicines may still be hidden in the rainforests of the world. As a result, over 100 companies that manufacture drugs are searching for new rainforest plants and testing them for possible medical use.

75　Unfortunately, access to these rainforest plants is rapidly disappearing. Logging companies are cutting down the rainforest trees and selling the wood. Commercial developers are laboring hard to clear the land for houses, 80 farms, towns, and roads. Clearly, the priorities of the scientists conflict with the priorities of the business people. The scientists want time to find plants that might cures diseases. The businesspeople want to make money from the 85 plants that grow there.

Experts believe that about 50,000 species[2] of plants, animals, and insects disappear every year because rainforests are being destroyed. Scientists fear that when rainforest species 90 disappear, many possible cures for diseases will disappear with them. They also fear that when rainforests disappear, the villages of native people who reside there will also disappear. When the people leave, their healers also leave. 95 These practitioners are the only individuals who know the secrets of healing sick people with forest plants.

In fact, most modern drugs made from plants came from simple cures that village 100 healers created from nearby plants. As a result, modern drug companies are sending scientists, accompanied by local translators, to work cooperatively with these village healers to learn their secrets before those secrets are lost 105 forever. Drug companies are also sending teams of workers into the rainforests to gather plants to test. If company scientists find a useful cure in a plant they test, they will identify the chemicals in the plant. Then, the company 110 can manufacture a medicine that is chemically identical.

Before rainforests disappear completely, scientists want to gather as many medical secrets as possible. Soon, however, it may be too late to 115 learn the rainforest's secrets.

---

[2] *species*: a group of living thing that differs from other groups

READING COMPREHENSION

Mark each sentence as *T*(true) or *F*(false) according to the information in Reading 2. Use your dictionary to check the meaning of new words.

.... 1. In 1633, Indians residing in Peru treated malaria with a powder made from tree bark.

.... 2. Europeans had access to quinine over 2,000 years ago.

.... 3. The discovery of *artemisinin* occurred in the 1960s.

.... 4. Taxol is now used in the intensive treatment of malaria.

.... 5. Drug companies are implementing searches in the rainforests for new medicinal plants.

.... 6. Logging companies are cooperating with scientists by cutting down trees.

.... 7. The priorities of rainforest loggers conflict with the priorities of developers.

.... 8. Translators accompany scientists into the rainforests to help scientists learn secrets from village healers.

.... 9. As rainforests disappear, the number of people living there will decline.

READING STRATEGY

Sometimes the title of an article can help you determine its main idea. Be sure to look at the title when you're trying to determine the main idea of an article.

The main idea of an article, or of the paragraphs within an article, is not always stated clearly in one sentence. Sometimes you have to add or remove words.

Answer these questions about the main idea of Reading 2 and the main ideas of the paragraphs.

1. Does the title "Searching for New Medicines" help you find the main idea of the article in the first paragraph? What is the main idea? Write it here in your own words.

   ....

2. The main idea of paragraph 2 is its first sentence. Take out the unnecessary words and write the main idea here.

   ....

3. Complete the main idea of paragraph 3:
   The ancient people of .... *had used* ....

4. Complete the main idea of paragraph 4:
   Aspirin was first used ....

5. Complete the main idea of paragraph 5:
   Taxol is an example of ....

6. Complete the main idea of paragraph 7:
   Access to ....

7. Write the main idea of paragraph 8 in your own words.

   ....

STEP I VOCABULARY ACTIVITIES: Word Level

A. Match each item in the first column with the thing that it usually accompanies. Then, tell a partner how the two things are connected.

.... 1. operating instructions   **a.** a new shirt

.... 2. dosage instructions   **b.** a frozen pizza

.... 3. laundering instructions   **c.** a computer program

.... 4. cooking instructions   **d.** a bottle of aspirin

.... 5. watering instructions   **e.** an electronic appliance

.... 6. installation instructions   **f.** a flowering plant

B. Use the target vocabulary from the box to complete this story. The words in parentheses can help you.

access to	declined	occurred	priority
accompanied	labored	practitioners	resided

Ignaz Semmelweis received his medical degree in Vienna in 1844. He took a job as head of a hospital department where women went to give birth to their babies. After giving birth, the new mothers .... in one of two large rooms while
(1. *lived*)
they recovered. In one of the rooms, many new mothers died of childbed fever, an infection inside their bodies that often .... childbirth many years ago.
(2. *went along with*)
In the second room, few women died. Semmelweis tried to understand why more deaths .... in the first room. Some people blamed bad air, but
(3. *happened*)
Semmelweis noticed that the first room was very dirty. The second room was very clean. He reasoned that something in the dirt was causing the infection. Semmelweis .... for weeks to improve the first room. Cleanliness became a
(4. *worked hard*)
....
(5. *matter of great importance*)
Doctors wearing bloody clothes could not have .... the patients.
(6. *contact with*)
Nurse .... and doctors had to wash their hands with a strong
(7. *workers*)
chemical before examining patients. Soon, the death rate .... in the
(8. *went down*)
first room.

The word *decline* usually refers to something becoming weaker, slower, or not as good.

> Grandfather's health is **declining**. (verb)

> His doctor noticed a **decline** in his weight. (noun)

Note: The verb *decline* is also used to reject or refuse something; for example, *decline an invitation*, or *decline to answer questions*.

C. Which of these things usually decline as a person grows older? Put a check (✓) next to them. Discuss why you checked these items with a partner.

.... eyesight   .... income   .... amount of sleep needed

.... doctor visits   .... TV viewing   .... time spent with family

.... intelligence   .... appetite   .... sense of humor

.... energy level   .... interests   .... patience

As a verb, *access* means "to get or use something."

> Doctors need to **access** patient information when they are treating an illness.

> I couldn't **access** my email.

As a noun, the word usually occurs in the phrase *have access to* something, which means "to be able to get or use something".

> Patients need to **have access to** information about the drugs they are taking.

The adjective form is often used in relation to people who lack certain abilities.

> These bathrooms are **accessible** to students in wheelchairs.

or

> These bathrooms are wheelchair **accessible**.

D. With a partner, decide which of these items should be accessible or inaccessible to small children. Write *A* for items that should be accessible and *I* for items that should be inaccessible. Give reasons for your answers.

.... scissors   .... other children   .... education

.... parks   .... battery-operated toys   .... electrical toys

.... stairs   .... their medicines   .... the bathroom water faucet

E. When do these things occur? How often do they recur? Discuss your answers with a partner.

1. New Year's Day
2. the first day of a class
3. a full moon
4. midnight
5. your birthday
6. a big family gathering
7. someone's wedding
8. chicken pox

STEP II VOCABULARY ACTIVITIES: Sentence Level

F. Think about these groups of people. Why might they have to cooperate with each other? Use your imagination and think of at least one reason for each group.

1. two scientists from different drug companies
2. the prime ministers of two different countries
3. two groups of students from different schools
4. two small children looking for sweets in the kitchen

In a small group, discuss these questions: How would the people probably feel about their cooperation? Would they have cooperative attitudes or hostile attitudes towards each other and the activity?

The verb *implement* means "to start using a plan, system, etc." The noun *implement* means "tool."

G. What are some examples of each of these implements? List as many examples as you can. Discuss your ideas with a partner.

1. a writing implement: ....

2. an eating implement: ....

3. a cutting implement: ....

4. a cleaning implement: ....

H. Imagine that you are a newspaper reporter interviewing the national Minister of Health about a new plan to control malaria in his country. Write questions to ask him using the words provided in any form. Be prepared to read your questions to the class or act out your interview with a partner.

1. implement: ....

2. access: ....

3. medical: ....

4. reside: ....

5. cooperate: ....

I. Self-Assessment Review: Go back to page 15 and reassess your knowledge of the target vocabulary. How has your understanding of the words changed? What words do you feel most comfortable with now?

WRITING AND DISCUSSION TOPICS

1. Reading 1 describes the cycle of malaria: from mosquito to person and back to mosquito. Describe another cycle of malaria: how malaria intensifies poverty and how poverty intensifies malaria.

2. When people do not know the real cause of an illness, they often create a cause, such as "bad air." They sometimes invent their own cures. What do you know about an old belief or cure? How did you learn about it? Did you ever try it? What happened?

3. Some people think that people today take too many medicines. They believe that some of these medicines hurt our bodies instead of helping them. Do you agree? What kinds of medicines do you think are necessary? Are there others that you think are not necessary?

4. Do you believe that medical care should be provided to all citizens by the government of a country? Why or why not? What problems might occur when the government runs the healthcare system, or when the government doesn't run the healthcare system?

THEY KNOW WHAT YOU WANT

In this unit, you will

- ➲ read about marketing strategy.
- ➲ read about how products are named.
- ➲ learn how to scan a text for specific information.
- ➲ increase your understanding of the target academic words for this unit:

administrate	domestic	implicit	invoke	sex
channel	explicit	income	publish	survey
convince	export	innovate	sector	

SELF-ASSESSMENT OF TARGET WORDS

Think carefully about how well you know each target word in this unit. Then, write it in the appropriate column in the chart.

I have never seen the word before.	I have seen the word but am not sure what it means.	I understand the word when I see or hear it in a sentence.	I have tried to use this word, but I am not sure I am using it correctly.	I use the word with confidence in either speaking *or* writing.	I use the word with confidence, both in speaking *and* writing.

MORE WORDS YOU'LL NEED

gimmick: something unusual or amusing that is used to attract people's attention, often for the purpose of selling something

BEFORE YOU READ

Read these questions. Discuss your answers in a small group.

1. Where do you see advertisements? Think of as many types of places as you can. Where do you see the most ads?

2. Has an advertisement ever persuaded you to buy a product?

3. If you invented a new product, what do you think would be the best way to introduce it to buyers?

READ

This introduction to a marketing textbook discusses the different ways that marketing reaches customers.

They Know What You Want

With her shopping list in hand, a supermarket customer is facing the challenge of selecting a breakfast cereal for her family. The shelves are stocked with as many as 200 varieties. Should
5 she buy wheat, corn, rice, bran, or oat cereal? Sweetened or plain? With added vitamins? With a plastic animal in the box? (Her kids would like that.) Or should she buy the one she has a coupon[1] for, or the one with the funny ad on TV,
10 or the one that is on sale?

The shopper's ultimate choice is likely to be determined by some factor other than taste. Marketers create gimmicks to entice shoppers to buy one product instead of another. Often
15 these have little to do with the food inside the boxes. They are only to attract shoppers.

Marketing is a company's plan for selling a product. A marketing plan, **administered** by a marketing director, includes what to name
20 the product, how to advertise it, how to price it, how to package it, and how to **convince** customers to buy it. In short, the goal of marketing is to **channel** a shopper's choices toward a single, specific product.

25 A marketing plan often begins with a **survey** to determine who is most likely to buy a certain type of product. Factors such as the **sex**, age, education, and **income** of future customers are considered. Then, a marketing team
30 designs a plan aimed at a specific **sector** of the population, the group that they think is most likely to buy the product.

Selling a perfume, a lawn mower, a ballpoint pen, and a pet food will obviously call for
35 different marketing techniques. Sex appeal may sell perfumes but not pens, while humor may sell pens, but not perfumes. Reliable performance sells lawn mowers and pens, but not pet food. Rich people buy expensive
40 perfumes. Students buy pens. Marketing teams must consider such factors when they design a marketing campaign.

Suppose that a company has developed an **innovative** new product: it is a powder made

---

[1] *coupon*: a small piece of paper from the company offering a discount on one of their products

from dried fruit. When mixed with warm water, the powder becomes a creamy fruit sauce for babies. Although babies will be the ones to eat the product, it is their parents who will buy it. The company's marketing plan will be aimed at the parents, specifically the mothers.

A survey indicates that most mothers have two top priorities: 1. they want their babies to be healthy; 2. they want to be good mothers. Marketers use this information to create a name for the new baby food: Healthy Start. They also create a marketing slogan: *Give your baby a Healthy Start*. This slogan has both an **explicit** and an **implicit** message. It explicitly directs a mother to feed a Healthy Start meal to her baby. It also implies that this will make her a good mother because she will be giving her baby a healthy start in life.

The marketing team then decides how and where to sell Healthy Start baby fruit. They must decide where to **publish** advertisements and what the ads should say. Maybe the ads will **invoke** the authority of a famous baby doctor to emphasize the health appeal. The ads will certainly emphasize things like good taste, easy preparation, and high nutrition. Maybe the ads will include coupons for free samples.

Maybe the marketing team will try something innovative, like offering a Healthy Start college scholarship to a lucky winner. The team must also decide if the focus will be on **domestic** sales or if the baby food will be **exported** to foreign countries. A design company is already designing an attractive package for the product. The marketing team will test the name, slogan, ads, and packaging by showing them to mothers and surveying their responses.

Finally, the new product will be placed on supermarket shelves. If the marketing was effective, mothers will select Healthy Start from the dozens of baby foods on the shelves.

READING COMPREHENSION

Mark each sentence as *T* (True) or *F* (False) according to the information in Reading 1. Use your dictionary to check the meaning of new words.

.... **1.** A marketing director administers a marketing plan.

.... **2.** A marketing plan includes ways to convince shoppers to buy a product.

.... **3.** Sex, age, income, and education are some of the factors that divide the population into different sectors.

.... **4.** A survey of mothers indicates that they want to be happy and want their babies to be smart.

.... **5.** A marketing slogan can have both an explicit and an implicit message.

.... **6.** Ads published in magazines might invoke the authority of a famous woman who is also a mother.

.... **7.** Marketing teams only think about domestic sales of their products.

.... **8.** Offering a scholarship would be an innovative gimmick for a new product.

READING STRATEGY: Scanning

Students often need to find specific information from a text that they already read. Rather than reread the entire text, you can *scan* the article to find the information you need. *Scanning* means quickly passing your eyes over a text to notice specific things.

Think about what to scan for in order to find specific information:

To find . . .	scan the text for . . .
names	capital letters
dates	numbers and capital letters
statistics	numbers and symbols
lists	a set of words separated by commas
specific words	capital letters, letter combinations, *italic* or **bold** words

Scan Reading 1 for the answers to these questions. Before you scan, decide what you should scan for in each case.

1. How many types of cereal does the supermarket sell? ....

2. What factors are considered in a survey? ....

3. What is one top priority for mothers? ....

4. What is the other top priority for mothers? ....

5. What is the name of the product? ....

6. What is the slogan for the product? ....

7. Will the marketing team export the product? ....

STEP I VOCABULARY ACTIVITIES: Word Level

A. Use the target vocabulary in the box to complete these analogies. Then, write the type of relationship each analogy has: example, synonym, antonym, action, or part (see Unit 1, page 11, for more on analogies). Compare answers with a partner.

administer	implicit	sex
export	income	publish

Relationship

1. red : color AS female : ....

2. radio program : broadcast AS newspaper : ....

3. take in : import AS send out : ....

4. direct : indirect AS explicit : ....

5. find : discover AS manage : ....

6. spend : money AS earn : ....

B. Read this marketing report. Use the target vocabulary in the box to complete the report. Compare your results with a partner.

> administrators implicit sexism
> domestic published surveys
> explicit sector

.... (1. *studies*) show that the .... (2. *part*) of society that washes the most dishes consists of women with children. Accordingly, marketing

.... (3. *managers*) target that sector when they design advertisements for a dishwashing liquid. The ads are .... (4. *printed*) alongside other ads for

.... (5. *home*) products in magazines that women primarily read. Ads like these often show a smiling woman washing dishes.

Many women feel that such ads show .... (6. *bias against one sex*). The women acknowledge that the .... (7. *clear and direct*) meaning is true: the soap *does* clean your dishes. They believe, however, that the .... (8. *hidden and indirect*) message is that washing dishes is a woman's job.

To *channel* something means "to make something move along a particular path or route." A *channel* is the path or route. It is often used to describe water or communications pathways. A television station is also called a *channel*.

*The police **channeled** traffic around the accident and onto side streets.*

*This area has flood **channels** that carry rainwater to the ocean.*

*If we can't settle this conflict, we will go through legal **channels** to find an answer.*

***Channel** 5 has the best local news programming.*

C. Choose one item from each column to create logical examples of a channel. Then, tell a partner how the ideas are connected.

Signs channel hotel guests to the right rooms.

~~signs~~	food and drinks	to the heart
airlines	donations	to a customer's table
waiters	~~hotel guests~~	to needy families
arteries and veins	passengers	~~to the right room~~
charities	blood	down the aisle to their seats

D. Where would you go to conduct a survey containing these questions? Why? Discuss your ideas with a partner.

1. *How much do you usually spend on groceries each week?* .... a grocery store ....

2. *What do you plan to do when you graduate?* ....

3. *What kind of books do you like to read?* ....

4. *What is your favorite ride at Disneyland?* ....

5. *Why do you ride a bus to work?* ....

6. *What is your biggest complaint about air travel?* ....

STEP II VOCABULARY ACTIVITIES: Sentence Level

Word Form Chart			
Noun	Verb	Adjective	Adverb
innovation innovator	innovate	innovative	innovatively

E. Complete this story using different forms of *innovate*.

Marketers know that .... advertising is one way to get the attention of buyers. This means that effective marketers try to ....
when they create a marketing plan. One .... created a process to print ads on the shells of eggs. Egg farmers did not want to pay for this
.... Grocery stores didn't either. Finally, a TV station agreed to pay to have their programs advertised on eggs.

It's too soon to know if this .... will successfully sell other products. One shopper complained, "Don't .... with my eggs! I have to eat those things!"

When a person or evidence persuades you, then you are *convinced*. The arguments or evidence was *convincing*.

*I read a **convincing** article about global warming. I'm **convinced** it's real.*

*The witnesses at the trial were **unconvincing**. I'm still **unconvinced** that they saw what happened.*

F. Restate these sentences in your notebook, using the form of *convince* in parentheses. Compare sentences with a partner.

1. Health professionals believe that obesity is a serious problem. (*are convinced*)

   Health professionals are convinced that obesity is a serious problem.

2. They want people to change the way they eat. (*convince*)

3. They have good evidence that junk foods are to blame. (*convincing*)

4. Food companies advertise in a believable way that junk foods are something people should eat all the time. (*convincingly*)

5. Children are especially easy to persuade. (*convince*)

6. Even if an ad shows something impossible to believe, children think it is real information. (*unconvincing*)

7. Food companies do not believe that they are to blame for children's obesity. (*unconvinced*)

8. They believe it is the parents' responsibility to control their children's diet. (*unconvinced*)

To *export* something means to send it to another country and sell it there. An *export* is the thing to sell. An *exporter* is a person in the business of exporting things.

*Brazil **exports** coffee around the world.*

*Tea is one of China's most important **exports**.*

***Exporters** look for inexpensive ways to transport their goods.*

Exported and *exporting* can be used as adjectives.

*Many of Mexico's **exported** goods go to the United States.*

*People in the **exporting** business need to speak several languages.*

G. Rewrite these headlines from the business section of the newspaper as complete sentences. Use a form of *export* in each sentence. Be prepared to read aloud or discuss your sentences in class.

1. German Autos Grew 14% in 2006

   The export of German automobiles grew 14% in 2006.

2. South Korea Sends 50,686 Cars to Russia in 2004

3. Honda and Toyota Make Japan Tops in Overseas Sales

4. Italy Delivers Fiats Globally

5. More Than Half U.S. Cars from Outside, Report Shows

6. Volkswagen Germany's Best Seller

7. Sending Saabs to Asia Good for Sweden

BEFORE YOU READ

Read these questions. Discuss your answers in a small group.

1. Many automobiles are named for animals, such as Cougar or Mustang. Would you buy an automobile named Turtle? How about Elephant? Why or why not?

2. What factors would you consider if you were responsible for naming a new product?

3. Does the name of a new product help you decide whether to try it? Why or why not?

READ

This excerpt from a marketing textbook discusses the factors that go into choosing a good name for a new product.

What's in a Name?

One of the most important tasks in marketing a new product is giving it a name. In terms of marketing, the quality of a product is not as important as the quality of the name it is given. This is because marketing is not about the product; it is about *selling* the product. Marketers use strategies such as attractive packaging, catchy slogans, and other gimmicks to convince consumers to buy their product. The most powerful marketing strategy, however, is giving a product a powerful name.

To be powerful, the name must be easy to remember. In the early days of computers, there were several competing brands on the market, including Apple II, Commodore Pet, IMSAI 8080, MITS Altair 8800, and Radio Shack TRS-80. In those days, most buyers knew very little about computers, so they were not able to judge the quality of one over the other. As a result, they rejected the computers with complex names. Instead, they chose the brands that invoked familiar ideas. They chose, of course, the Apple II.

The name must also be easy to pronounce. If customers can't pronounce the name of a product, they won't buy it. A short name is easier to remember and to pronounce. According to research done by Strategic Name Development consultants, the best names have three or fewer syllables, such as Tums (antacid tablets), Xerox (copiers), or Cheerios (cereal). Many well-known names are longer, of course, such as Energizer (batteries) and Coca Cola (soft drinks), so length is not the only factor.

A product name should be unique. It shouldn't sound like the name of any other product, especially a competing product. Shoppers tend to confuse Breyer's Ice Cream with Dreyer's Ice Cream and Rolex (watches) with Rolodex (desk indexes), for example.

In addition, an effective name should hint at what the product is used for. For example, Sleepeez is a sleeping medication and Windex is a window cleaner. A name should also be appropriate for the type of product it represents. Names of medicines should sound medical, names of foods should sound tasty, and names of domestic cleaning products should sound hard-working.

An effective name also includes words, or parts of words, that are positive and inviting. Sometimes, the product name sounds like another descriptive word that has a positive meaning. The pain reliever Aleve, for example, sounds like "relieve." Band-Aid (a small plastic bandage) includes the word "aid." Frequently, names of products aimed at high-income consumers implicitly advertise luxury. Consider the names of these cruise ship companies: Crystal, Princess, Royal Caribbean, and Celebrity.

The letters within names are important, too. A survey administered by the above consultants asked English speakers about their reactions to various letters of the alphabet. The results showed that people associate the letters C, S, and B with something traditional, but associate the letters Q, V, X, and Z with something innovative. Additionally, people in the survey associated certain letters with one sex or the other. They considered the letters F, L, V, and W feminine, but the letters M, X, and Z masculine. It is not clear how those surveyed might react to the automobile names Volvo, Mazda, or Lexus.

Marketers must also consider how a product name will translate in other languages if the product is exported. When the Chevrolet Nova automobile was exported to Argentina in the 1970s, some people predicted that it would sell poorly because in Spanish the two words "No va" mean "It doesn't go." Fortunately, "nova" (a bright star) is the same word in both Spanish and English.

Finally, a name must not generate negative associations in the minds of consumers. Many words have an implicit message as well as an explicit meaning. Why, for example, has no car manufacturer named a car the Elephant? Elephants are big, strong, and dependable, but they are also slow-moving, fat, and eat a lot. There used to be a weight-loss product called Aids. It disappeared once AIDS became a serious illness worldwide.

Corporations put forth great effort to find the right name for a new product. They often hire consultants who specialize in creating product names. Working with the principles above, they create several possible names. Then, they channel the names through one or more focus groups. These groups are made up of individuals drawn from the sector of the population that is most likely to buy the target product, such as, dog owners, frequent travelers, or senior citizens. When a focus group meets, they freely discuss what they like or don't like about the possible names.

Once the right name is chosen, advertisements are widely published to introduce the new product to the buying public. Only time will tell if the important marketing decisions made earlier will be effective in selling the product.

READING COMPREHENSION

.... 1. A powerful name helps convince consumers to buy a product.

.... 2. Early computer buyers chose a brand name that invoked high-tech innovation.

.... 3. The names of domestic cleaning products should sound hard-working.

.... 4. Many words have an implicit message as well as an explicit meaning.

.... 5. A survey administered by naming consultants showed that product names spelled with an X are considered innovative.

.... 6. A product name must be changed if the product is exported to other countries.

.... 7. High-income car buyers would be likely to buy a luxury car named Elephant.

.... 8. Naming consultants channel possible product names through focus groups drawn from the sector of the population most likely to buy the target product.

READING STRATEGY

A. Scanning is useful for finding examples. Scan Reading 2 to find this information.

1. the number of products names that include an X: ....

2. the number of product names that include a V: ....

3. the number of product names that include a Z: ....

B. Scan the article again to find out what kind of product each of these is or was.

1. Celebrity ....

2. Pet ....

3. Aleve ....

4. Rolodex ....

5. Aids ....

6. Windex ....

7. Cheerios ....

8. Nova ....

9. Tums ....

10. Energizer ....

STEP I VOCABULARY ACTIVITIES: Word Level

To *invoke* can mean simply to ask for help or support from someone, especially a spiritual being. More commonly, it is used when someone wants to cite an authority to support an action or opinion.

*The professor **invoked** several leading scholars to support his arguments.*

Advertisements often invoke the authority of powerful people or institutions to convince customers to buy their product.

*The signs in the bookstore for this new dictionary **invoke** the authority of professors from several different university programs.*

A. Read these ads and decide what products they might be advertising. Discuss your choices with a partner. Then, together, think of another type of product and write an ad for it. Be sure to invoke a convincing authority.

1. "When the U.S. Olympic hockey team needs a burst of energy, they grab a *Champ* and keep on going!"

   Product: ....

2. "Celebrity chef Michelangelo Sotto uses only the best ingredients in his spaghetti sauce. That's why he uses new *Multo, Multo*."

   Product: ....

3. "Scholars and academics across the country turn to *WordPower*—because accuracy matters."

   Product: ....

4. "The American Association of Children's Dentists recommends *Glisten* over all other competitors."

Product: ....

5. "Hollywood actresses have to look their best. That's why Hollywood's best make-up artists choose *Azure* products."

Product: ....

6. "Formula One drivers depend on *Nexosol*—the fuel of champions!"

Product: ....

7. Product: ....

Ad: ....

....

As everyone knows, *sex* refers to intimate contact. Based on this core meaning, there are many word forms, uses, and collocations.

Sex refers to the state of being male or female. In this sense, *gender* has the same meaning.

> *Most parents want children of both **sexes**. They don't prefer one gender over the other.*

Sexuality refers to the awareness of being one sex or the other. The adjective is *sexual*.

> *Children pay no attention to **sexuality** until about the age of three.*

> *Most children reach **sexual** maturity by the time they are 16.*

Sexism is a social bias against people of one sex. The adjective is *sexist*. *Sexist* is also a noun for the person who has this bias.

> *Although **sexism** is against the law in workplaces, many companies have **sexist** policies that favor male administrators.*

> *The politician was accused by coworkers of being a **sexist**.*

B. Match these expressions that use the word *sex* with their definitions. Compare answers with a partner.

.... **1.** the opposite sex   **a.** an old-fashioned label for women

.... **2.** sexual harassment   **b.** a person, usually a celebrity, known mostly for his or her attractiveness

.... **3.** the fairer sex   **c.** serving the needs of either gender

.... **4.** sex symbol   **d.** attractiveness to others on a physical level

.... **5.** sex appeal   **e.** the gender that someone is not

.... **6.** unisex   **f.** using someone's gender against them in some way, usually in the workplace

Word Form Chart			
Noun	Verb	Adjective	Adverb
sex(es) sexuality sexism	....	sexual	sexually
....	....	explicit	explicitly
....	....	implicit	implicitly

C. Read this paragraph about sexuality and marketing. Complete the sentences with a form of *sex, implicit,* or *explicit.* Compare answers with a partner.

One thing that humans of both (1) s... fear is that they will not be able to attract a mate. Marketers use this fear. They know that (2) s... suggestive ads can convince people that a particular product will help them attract a mate. However, marketers must be careful. Ads cannot be too (3) e... because that upsets some consumers. As a result, ads seldom (4) e... use (5) s... to sell a product. Instead, they (6) i... suggest that a product will make consumers more attractive to the opposite (7) s... . To appeal to women, for example, a magazine ad for contact lenses might show the face of a woman with beautiful eyes. The caption reads, "He'll love what he sees," but the (8) i... message is, "He'll love *you* if you wear our contact lenses." An ad targeted at men might show a strong, confident man driving a sports car with a beautiful woman next to him. There are no words, but the picture (9) i... suggests two things. If you drive this car, you'll be strong and confident, too—and beautiful women will be yours.

STEP II VOCABULARY ACTIVITIES: Sentence Level

> Domestic refers to the home and family or to a home country. It can be used in many different contexts.
>
> *You'll find cleaning products and implements in the "**Domestic** Needs" aisle of the supermarket.*
>
> ***Domestic** postal rates are lower than overseas rates.*
>
> *My country exports 25% of **domestically** grown fruits and vegetables.*
>
> *Scientists say that **domesticated** animals live longer than wild animals.*

D. Rewrite these sentences in your notebook using a form of *domestic*. Compare sentences with a partner.

1. Nowadays, husbands are more likely to help their wives with household chores.

   Nowadays, husbands are more likely to help their wives with domestic chores.

2. Dog lovers think of their pets as family members rather than as tame animals.

3. A "white sale" is when products for the home, such as towels and sheets, are on sale.

4. You should arrive at the airport two hours before flights within the country.

5. Coffee must be imported from other countries because it is not grown here.

> To *administer* means to control and manage the giving of something, for example, a doctor administers medicine to patients, or a teacher administers a test to students. The most common usage of this word family, however, is for business and politics:
>
> *administrator*   a manager in a company, organization, or government
> *administration*   the work done by administrators
> *the administration*   the group of people managing an organization or government
>
> *The school **administrator** was pleased with the success of the innovative programs she has implemented across the city.*
>
> *The director oversaw the **administration** of the new safety rules.*
>
> ***The administration** has been criticized for wasting taxpayers' money.*
>
> Administrative refers to the work of administering services, or office work in general. *Administratively* is the adverb.
>
> *The chief of police has an **administrative** role in the police department.*
>
> *My brother is the **administrative** assistant for the whole department.*
>
> *The fire department is **administratively** separate from the city government.*

E. Read the chart showing some of the employees of Black's Button Company. Then, answer the questions that follow in your notebook. Include the form of *administer* indicated in each sentence.

Name	Title	Area of Responsibility
Jerry Green	Plant Manager	safety and maintenance of the factory
Marie Brown	Administrative Assistant	secretary to Fred Black
Fred Black	Chief Executive Officer	operation of the entire company
Ellen White	Marketing Director	marketing
Jane Gray	Human Resources Director	employment office

1. What does Marie Brown do? (*administratively*)

    She assists Mr. Black administratively.

2. Who is Fred Black? (*administrator*)
3. What does Ellen White do? (*administrative responsibility*)
4. What does Jane Gray do? (*administers*)
5. What does Jerry Green do? (*administration*)

F. Which of the jobs in the chart in activity E would you be best at? Why? What are your administrative strengths and weaknesses? Write a short paragraph in which you explain your answers. Be prepared to present your work in class.

G. Self-Assessment Review: Go back to page 29 and reassess your knowledge of the target vocabulary. How has your understanding of the words changed? What words do you feel most comfortable with now?

WRITING AND DISCUSSION TOPICS

1. Survey students of both sexes to find out what they drink at breakfast. First, survey the class and tally the results in a chart (see below). Then, find ten people outside of class and ask them the same question. Tally those results and compare them with the class results. Write a paragraph that summarizes the whole survey.

	Coffee	Tea	Milk	Water	Juice	Soft Drink
Men						
Women						

2. Reading 2 mentions several rules for naming a product. Think of some successful products whose names do not follow these rules. Why do you think they are successful anyway?

3. Find an advertisement that you like in a magazine. Who do you think is the target market? How does this ad try to convince the target market to buy the product? Is it innovative in some way? If so, how?

4. Describe a television ad that you don't like. Why don't you like it? What product was being advertised? Would you consider buying the product? Why or why not?

Unit 4 Sociology

WHAT YOUR CLOTHES SAY ABOUT YOU

In this unit, you will

- ⊃ read about clothing and its meaning.
- ⊃ learn how to identify examples in a text.
- ⊃ increase your understanding of the target academic words for this unit:

acquire	civil	convene	integral	style
ambiguous	constitute	differentiate	military	via
analogy	context	index	somewhat	whereby

SELF-ASSESSMENT OF TARGET WORDS

Think carefully about how well you know each target word in this unit. Then, write it in the appropriate column in the chart.

I have never seen the word before.	I have seen the word but am not sure what it means.	I understand the word when I see or hear it in a sentence.	I have tried to use this word, but I am not sure I am using it correctly.	I use the word with confidence in either speaking *or* writing.	I use the word with confidence, both in speaking *and* writing.

BEFORE YOU READ

Read these questions. Discuss your answers in a small group.

1. Do you think it's important to wear clothes that are in style?
2. Why are clothes important to people?
3. How do you decide what kind of clothing to buy for yourself?

READ

This magazine article tells about how people's clothing conveys a great deal of information about them.

What Your Clothes Say About You

People wear clothes to protect their bodies from the cold or the burning sun, from insect bites and injuries, and from the unwelcome eyes of strangers. However, what people wear can
5 also convey a message about who they are and their role in society.

For example, visit nearly any country in the world and you will notice that young people everywhere are wearing fashionable blue jeans,
10 not for work, but for social occasions such as parties and concerts. The jeans are **somewhat** of an **index** of how these young people view themselves: *I'm modern and stylish. I'm relaxed and confident. I'm different from the traditional*
15 *older generation. I'm sexy.* Jeans make such an important statement that, in some groups, a person might be judged by the brand of jeans he or she is wearing. As a result, some young people feel pressured into spending hundreds of dollars
20 to **acquire** a single pair of designer jeans just to be in fashion.

An even more direct means **whereby** people make statements about themselves is **via** messages printed on T-shirts. One says *Oxford*
25 *University*. Another reads *Italy 2006 World Cup*. There are many kinds of T-shirt messages. They can convey allegiance to schools and sports teams, advertise places or products, make political statements, serve as wearable
30 travel souvenirs, and commemorate important

occasions. These wearable messages are seldom **ambiguous**. They clearly tell others, *This is what I want you to know about me.*

Clothes mark people as part of a group.

Just as blue jeans and T-shirts say a great deal
35 about the people who are wearing them, so does the Western business suit. It says that the person wants to impress others with his or her professional status. A fitted jacket and matching trousers **constitute** a man's suit, while a fitted
40 jacket and matching skirt constitute a woman's suit. A collared shirt and a necktie are **integral** parts of the man's outfit, while stockings and high-heeled shoes complete the woman's. Often this attire is not what the person chooses to
45 wear, but it is what a company requires its top-level employees to wear. The business suit is so conventional that it is **analogous** to a uniform in other occupations.

A uniform identifies the occupation of many
50 people. **Military** personnel are easy to identify by their uniforms. The same is true for **civil**

emergency personnel like police officers and fire fighters. Medical workers, airline pilots, and members of religious orders are other examples of people whose work can be identified by their clothing. In certain **contexts**, special clothing is worn to **differentiate** not only the occupation of people, but also their authority. For example, when a court of law **convenes**, the judge's robe is a clear indicator of her role and authority. Similarly, the chef's tall white hat indicates his job and that he's in charge in the restaurant's kitchen.

Clothing might also show which group a person belongs to. For example, Scotsmen wear distinctive tartans to show their clan affiliation, just as city street gangs wear colored headscarves to show their gang membership. Similarly, school uniforms identify children as students at a certain school.

Societies choose different ways to show marital status. In Western societies, women— and often men—wear wedding rings on their left hands. Other cultures use different symbols. Hindu women, for example, wear a red powder in their hair after they marry. Unmarried Amish women wear black bonnets on their heads, while married women wear white ones.

Clothing serves many functions beyond just protecting our bodies. Clothing can tell a lot about the people who wear it.

READING COMPREHENSION

Mark each sentence as *T* (true) or *F* (false) according to the information in Reading 1. Use your dictionary to check the meaning of new words.

.... 1. People send messages about themselves via what they wear.

.... 2. For many people, jeans are somewhat of an index of their identity.

.... 3. A young person might spend a few dollars to acquire a pair of designer jeans.

.... 4. T-shirt messages that show allegiance to a school or sports team are often ambiguous.

.... 5. A suit and necktie are integral parts of men's and women's business attire.

.... 6. A jacket and matching trousers constitute the uniforms of military personnel.

.... 7. Business suits are analogous to uniforms because both men and women wear them.

.... 8. Civil emergency personnel, such as police officers and fire fighters, are easily identified because they wear uniforms.

.... 9. When a court of law convenes, people can differentiate the judge from other people by her special clothing.

.... 10. Wearing veils of different colors is the means whereby Amish women show if they are married or unmarried.

READING STRATEGY: Identifying Examples

One way that writers make their ideas clear is by giving **examples**. Sometimes an entire text is made up of examples, with each paragraph giving a different kind of example to support the main idea of the reading. There can also be several examples within one paragraph to help explain the ideas in that paragraph.

Reading 1 uses examples in both these ways. The main idea of the reading is in paragraph 1: *What people wear can convey a message about who they are and their role in society*. Each paragraph that follows gives an example of a kind of clothing that conveys a message. In Paragraph 3, *Oxford University* is an example of the main idea of that paragraph—messages on T-shirts.

You can identify examples in a text by looking for certain signals. Some common words and phrases that signal examples are:

for example or *for instance*
like or *such as*
There are many kinds of . . .
One is . . . *Another is* . . .

Refer back to Reading 1 to answer these questions.

1. In each paragraph, what example of clothing conveys a message?

   Paragraph 2 .... blue jeans ....   Paragraph 5 ....

   Paragraph 3 ....   Paragraph 6 ....

   Paragraph 4 ....   Paragraph 7 ....

2. In Paragraph 3, identify the signals that introduce examples, and write them in the blanks.

   a. .... reads *Italy 2006 World Cup*.

   b. .... They can convey allegiance to schools and sports teams, advertise places or products, make political statements, serve as wearable travel souvenirs, and commemorate important occasions.

3. In Paragraph 5, list the examples of occupations that can be identified by clothing.

   ....

4. In Paragraph 7, which words introduce the examples of the Hindu women and Amish women?

   ....

STEP I VOCABULARY ACTIVITIES: Word Level

A. Use the target vocabulary in the box to complete this story. The words in parentheses can help you.

> acquired   conventional   via
> constituted   integral   whereby
> context   somewhat

In 1849, thousands of people went to California in search of gold, hoping to get rich. Levi Strauss, a cloth salesman, went there, too. He hoped to get rich, but in a different way. When the gold miners complained that their pants tore easily, Strauss made them pants out of strong denim cloth. The men liked the pants, but the pockets kept tearing. This .... a problem, but a tailor had an
(1. *made*)
idea .... the pockets could be made stronger with copper rivets.
(2. *by which*)
Strauss and the tailor soon became rich—not from gold, but from inventing jeans. For the next 100 years, jeans were worn mostly by farmers or factory workers. In the 1950s, young people began wearing jeans. They made a strong statement against
.... dress .... their jeans, but jeans were considered
(3. *standard*)   (4. *by means of*)
improper by most people. In the 1960s, jeans became .... more
(5. *a little*)
acceptable, and in the .... of the 1970s, they ....
(6. *setting*)   (7. *earned*)
fashion status. Today, jeans are an .... part of nearly every young
(8. *necessary*)
person's wardrobe.

> *Somewhat* has the same meaning as "sort of" or "a little bit."
>
> My sister is **somewhat** of a fashion expert.
>
> His trousers were **somewhat** wrinkled, and his shirt was torn.

B. Read the statements in the survey and mark your opinion in the appropriate column. Discuss your answers in a small group.

Statements	I strongly agree.	I somewhat agree.	I somewhat disagree.	I strongly disagree.
Women pay too much attention to clothes.				
Men don't pay enough attention to clothes.				

> *Via* means "passing through" or "by way of a place."
>
> *I'll fly from here to Berlin **via** Paris.*
>
> It can also mean "by means of" or "using."
>
> *Relatives who live far from each other can keep in touch **via** email.*

C. Imagine that you are the president of a large company. By what means would you communicate each of these messages to your employees? Match the messages on the left with the means on the right. Then, tell a partner the reasons for your answers.

.... 1. We've had a dangerous chemical spill.

.... 2. You haven't been doing your job. You're fired.

.... 3. Please sign this form and return it to me.

.... 4. There's a manager's meeting at 8 a.m. tomorrow.

.... 5. Please come to my office right away.

.... 6. Congratulations to Jim Smith on his new baby.

a. via a Post-it note

b. via email

c. via telephone

d. via a face-to-face discussion

e. via the company newsletter

f. via the public address system

> People in a society can be divided into three sectors: *military*, *religious*, and *civil*.
>
> *Members of the army, navy, and air force constitute the **military** sector.*
>
> *Men and women who devote their lives to worship constitute the **religious** sector.*
>
> *Ordinary citizens constitute the **civil** sector.*

D. Read the list of occupations. Write *M* for a military job, *R* for a religious job, and *C* for a civil title.

.... captain

.... firefighter

.... general

.... lawyer

.... librarian

.... manager

.... monk

.... nun

.... priest

.... soldier

STEP II VOCABULARY ACTIVITIES: Sentence Level

> To *differentiate* one thing from another means "to create a difference between them," or "to see the difference."
>
> *Designers **differentiate** between clothing for young women and older women.*
>
> *It's hard to **differentiate** between jeans for men and jeans for women.*
>
> The noun form is *differentiation*.
>
> ***Differentiation** between military ranks is shown by stripes on uniform sleeves.*

E. Complete this paragraph about athletic shoes, using the correct forms of *differentiate*.

Athletic shoes are designed for sports such as running, tennis, handball, and basketball. Manufacturers have .... shoes for each sport, but all shoes are designed to minimize impact on the bottom of the feet. One main difference is the amount of cushioning. A shoe with little cushioning is suitable for walking, ... it from a running shoe, which requires more cushioning. Microprocessors in some running shoes .... between hard and soft surfaces and automatically adjust how the shoe absorbs the impact.

> Something that is *ambiguous* is not clear in meaning, usually because there is more than one possible meaning. For example, the newspaper headline "Hospital Begins Operations" is *ambiguous*. The *ambiguity* is caused by the word "operations," which has more than one meaning. "Operations" can refer to either medical surgery or services.
>
> The headline can be rewritten to clarify the meaning that the writer wants to convey. Two *unambiguous* headlines are: "Hospital Begins Surgery" or "Hospital Opens for Service."

F. Read these ambiguous headlines, and underline the ambiguous word in each one. Then, write two unambiguous headlines for each item.

1. <u>Substitute</u> Found for TV Show

   Substitute Actor Hired for TV Show ....

   Cancelled TV Show Will Be Replaced ....

2. Rare Monkey Eats Carrots and Flies

   ....

   ....

3. Doctor Administers New Drug Test

   ....

   ....

4. Bus Riders Miss Streetcar

   ....

   ....

Now, tell a partner why each headline is ambiguous. Discuss how you rewrote the headlines to resolve the ambiguities.

To *convene* means "to meet or come together, usually for an official or formal meeting." The noun form is *convention*.

> The parliament **convenes** each morning at 10 a.m.

> I'll attend a medical **convention** in Tokyo next month.

Convention can also mean a tradition or a standard way of behaving.

> The Western **convention** is for a married woman to take her husband's surname.

Something *conventional* is traditional or standard, while something *unconventional* is unusual and often disapproved of.

> Teenagers often like to shock adults with **unconventional** clothes.

> They should dress **conventionally** when they apply for a job.

G. Write the answers to these questions in your notebook. Write in full sentences and use the word in parentheses.

1. Describe a common wedding tradition practiced in your family. (*conventionally*)

2. Describe the clothing worn by men and women students at your school. (*conventional*)

3. Describe where students at your school gather for meetings. (*convene*)

4. Describe a standard way that people greet each other. (*convention*)

Whereby means "by which" or "because of which." It is a formal way to connect two ideas. The first idea describes an action and the second part shows the result of the action.

> Nancy went on a strict diet **whereby** she lost 35 pounds.

Note that *whereby* connects two full clauses.

H. Match the clauses in the left column with those on the right to make logical sentences, using *whereby*. **Write the sentences in your notebook. Compare sentences with a partner.**

> Teens wear T-shirts and jeans, whereby they differentiate themselves from older people.

...*e*... **1.** Teens wear T-shirts and jeans   **a.** people can see new styles

.... **2.** Fashion editors create magazines   **b.** they can stay in cold water longer

.... **3.** One designer created all her clothes in black   **c.** women could be more comfortable

.... **4.** Early 20th century designers created looser styles   **d.** she built her reputation

.... **5.** Surfers are wearing new wet suits   **e.** they differentiate themselves from older people

BEFORE YOU READ

Read these questions. Discuss your answers in a small group.

1. What jobs or social roles require people to wear special clothing?
2. What clothes do you associate with royalty (kings and queens, etc.)?
3. A flag is one symbol of a nation. What are some other things that can be used as symbols of a nation?

READ

This excerpt from a social science textbook is about the significance of clothing as a signal of important ideas and values in a culture.

Symbolic Clothing

Hundreds of years ago, umbrellas were symbols of power and authority. Kings, sheikhs, popes, and other rulers believed that owning these sunshades added to their importance.
5 The more umbrellas a ruler had, the more he impressed others; and the bigger his umbrellas, the more power the owner appeared to have. It seems odd to us today that such an everyday object could have once been used to differentiate
10 rulers from ordinary people. Yet at that time, an umbrella was an unambiguous symbol of power. Similarly, contemporary cultures today employ many common things, including clothing, as symbols of social status.

15 For example, in the civil courts of law in many countries, judges wear long robes, usually black, that cover their ordinary clothing. The robes identify the judges' role in the courtroom and symbolize their authority to
20 administer justice. The gavel that judges rap to convene court and maintain order is another such symbol of authority. In Britain and in most Commonwealth nations, judges and certain court officials also wear white wigs that
25 symbolize their roles.

Similarly, the ceremonial clothing of European kings and queens is symbolic of their royal authority. Nowadays they wear the long, fur-trimmed capes only on special occasions, with
30 jeweled crowns on their heads and jeweled staffs, called scepters, held in their hands.

The academic cap and gown is another example of symbolic clothing. Hundreds of years ago, students at European universities
35 were required to wear long, black robes. Today academic robes are worn only for graduation ceremonies along with a close-fitting black cap topped by a flat, black square. A tassel, which is a bundle of long silk strings tied together,
40 hangs from a button in the center of the square. By convention, students begin the graduation ceremony with the tassel hanging from the right side of the square. Once a university administrator declares that the students have
45 officially graduated, they move their tassels to

Students move the tassels as a symbol of transition.

the left side of the square to indicate their new change of status. Graduating students also wear short drapes of cloth over their gowns, whereby their field of academic specialization is indicated
50 via color. An orange cloth symbolizes engineering, for example, and green symbolizes medicine.

A wedding, too, is a change-of-status ceremony. Traditional attire is an integral part of the ritual. In a conventional Western
55 wedding, the bride wears a long, white dress. She also wears a white veil on her head and carries a bouquet of flowers. Her clothing and various accessories (which may be hidden) constitute traditional good-luck items that a
60 bride should carry: "something old, something new, something borrowed, something blue, and a lucky penny in her shoe." An important part of the ceremony is the exchange of wedding rings. These circles of gold or silver have no ending,
65 and symbolize the lifetime relationship the bride and groom are about to begin.

The symbolism of the Western white wedding dress is so strong that brides from many non-Western cultures have chosen to include such
70 a dress in their weddings. An Asian bride, for example, might wear a red gown during a

Traditional Western wedding clothes are becoming popular everywhere.

traditional wedding ceremony and then change into a white wedding dress.

Unlike judges or royalty, who wear symbolic
75 clothing only for certain occasions, religious leaders tend to wear clothing that identifies their religious roles at all times. In many religions, there are two kinds of religious clothing. Religious leaders wear one kind of clothing on a daily basis as
80 they perform nonceremonial tasks. The other kind is what they wear while participating in religious ceremonies. Often this attire is a long robe of a certain color, perhaps decorated with religious symbols. In some religions, the leaders must wear
85 head coverings, while in others they are forbidden to cover their heads.

Military personnel, too, wear uniforms at all times, but different types. One type is for everyday wear, and another is the formal
90 uniform worn for military ceremonies. A third type is worn in battle. Military uniforms serve several symbolic functions. First, the various decorations on a uniform jacket and hat are indexes of someone's position in the military.
95 Second, uniforms encourage members of a group to acquire a sense of unity and pride. Finally, in the context of a battle, uniforms become symbols of the nation the soldiers are defending.

Symbolic clothing can symbolize many things,
100 including authority, nationality and change of status. Often the original significance of the clothing has been forgotten or has changed over time, yet societies continue to respect the symbolism. Other clothing, such as the white
105 wedding dress, became symbolic somewhat recently, yet is still considered traditional. The objects and clothing that become important symbols in a culture are determined by the special meaning that people give them.

READING COMPREHENSION

Mark each sentence as *T*(true) or *F*(false) according to the information in Reading 2. Use your dictionary to check the meaning of new words.

.... **1.** Hundreds of years ago, the umbrellas that kings, sheikhs, and popes acquired became indexes of their high positions in society.

.... **2.** Sometimes ambiguous symbols of power are used to differentiate between rulers and ordinary people.

.... **3.** The gavel that judges rap to convene sessions in a civil court of law is a symbol of the nation they represent.

.... **4.** Graduating students wear drapes of cloth over their academic gowns whereby they indicate their change of status via color.

.... **5.** A long white dress and a white veil constitute the wedding clothing of a traditional Western bride.

.... **6.** In some cultures, the Western wedding dress is becoming an integral part of non-Western wedding ceremonies.

.... **7.** In the context of a battle, uniforms become symbols of military rank.

.... **8.** The symbolism of some ceremonial clothing, such as the academic cap and gown, is somewhat recent.

READING STRATEGY

1. Reread the first paragraph of Reading 2. Find the sentence that tells you the main idea of the article, and write it here.

   ....

2. Each paragraph in the article discusses a different example of symbolic clothing. Who wears the symbolic clothing mentioned in each of these paragraphs?

   Paragraph 2 ....   Paragraph 6 ....

   Paragraph 3 ....   Paragraph 7 ....

   Paragraph 4 ....   Paragraph 8 ....

3. Paragraph 3 gives three examples of symbols of authority. What are they?

   ....

4. What three items constitute the traditional attire of a bride in a Western wedding?

   ....

5. In Paragraph 8, what words introduce three kinds of military uniforms?

   ....

6. What words introduce the three symbolic functions of military uniforms?

   ....

STEP I VOCABULARY ACTIVITIES: Word Level

> Sometimes creating an *analogy* takes imagination.
>
> *Some people see an **analogy** between the features on the outside of a house and a face. The windows are **analogous** to eyes, for example.*

A. How is an automobile like a person? Create an analogy by matching each car part in the left column with an analogous body part on the right.

.... **1.** engine
.... **2.** windshield
.... **3.** driver
.... **4.** tires
.... **5.** gasoline
.... **6.** car wash
.... **7.** gasoline tank

a. food
b. feet
c. heart
d. brain
e. bath
f. stomach
g. eyes

> An *index* is an indication or a measurement of something.
>
> *The consumer price **index** shows changes in the prices of products over time.*
>
> The *index* of a textbook helps readers locate information in the book.
>
> *Check the **index** of your science text to see if it covers cell division.*
>
> **Note:** *Indexes* is the common plural form, but sometimes *indices* is used.

B. Read these statements about an imaginary country. What might each statement be an index of? Discuss your answers in a small group.

1. Most people live to be 75 years old or more.
2. Most children of the residents go to college.
3. Almost every adult of working age has a job.
4. Ninety percent of the adults vote in elections.

C. When something is an *integral* part of a whole thing, it means that it is a necessary or required part. Complete these sentences. Refer to the information in Reading 2. Compare answers with a partner.

1. In some religions, ... is an integral part of a religious leader's ceremonial clothing.
2. Changing the .... is an integral part of a graduation ceremony.
3. Exchanging .... is an integral part of a Western wedding.
4. .... has become an integral part of some non-Western weddings.

STEP II VOCABULARY ACTIVITIES: Sentence Level

Word Form Chart			
Noun	Verb	Adjective	Adverb
context	contextualize	context contextualized	....

> One meaning of *context* is the "circumstance or situation in which something occurs."
>
> *A judge's robe is a symbol of authority only in the **context** of a courtroom.*
>
> *Context* can also refer to the words and ideas in a text that help readers understand new or ambiguous words. Good readers use *context clues* to help them understand new or ambiguous words in a text. It is hard to learn new words in a list because the words are not *contextualized*.
>
> *In Reading 2, the **context clues**—academic clothing, graduation ceremony, cap—help you understand what the word "tassel" means.*

D. Complete each of these sentences with information about the context. Compare your answers with a partner.

1. A business suit is the proper attire in a business context.
2. Soldiers' uniforms help differentiate friends from enemies ....
3. A head covering is often required ....
4. A chef is the boss ....

E. Each of these words has more than one meaning. Consult your dictionary to find the different meanings. Then, in your notebook, write a sentence that provides a context explaining <u>one</u> meaning of each word. Compare sentences in a small group.

1. refrain

   The guitarist sang the verses of the song and asked the audience to sing the refrain after each verse.

2. game
3. orange
4. gag
5. pale

The verb *constitute* means "to make up or form something." The adjective form is *constituent*.

> Nine players **constitute** a baseball team.
>
> The **constituent** parts of a woman's suit are a fitted jacket and matching skirt.

F. In your notebook, write sentences that tell the constituent parts of each of these things. Compare your answers with a partner.

1. a textbook
2. an orchestra
3. a first-aid kit
4. a computer
5. a soccer uniform

The verb *acquire* means "to obtain or gain something." You can acquire something physical (books, property, etc.) or abstract (knowledge, a skill, a habit, etc.).

> I **acquired** an antique violin recently.
>
> I **acquired** a good education in my small town school.

The noun form is *acquisition*.

> The violin is my most valuable **acquisition**.
>
> The **acquisition** of a second language is not easy.

G. Write a short paragraph about a real or imaginary trip that you took to a foreign country. Name at least four things that you acquired on your trip. Include the word *acquisition*. Be prepared to present your work in class.

H. Self-Assessment Review: Go back to page 43 and reassess your knowledge of the target vocabulary. How has your understanding of the words changed? What words do you feel most comfortable with now?

WRITING AND DISCUSSION TOPICS

1. "Clothes make the man" is an old saying. It means that what you wear shows the kind of person that you are. Do you agree or disagree?

2. Some people are accused of being "slaves to fashion." This means that they wear the latest style even if they don't like it or even if it does not flatter them. How important is it to be in style?

3. What are some reasons why sports teams wear uniforms?

4. Do you believe that school uniforms are a good idea, or should school children be allowed to choose their clothing?

5. Readings 1 and 2 describe several ways that people show their authority through clothes or other symbols. What are some other examples?

Unit 5 Psychology

SUCCESS STORY

In this unit, you will

- ➲ read about the meaning of success and how people achieve it.
- ➲ read about a personality disorder related to success.
- ➲ learn to identify definitions within a text.
- ➲ increase your understanding of the target academic words for this unit:

attain	colleague	dynamic	inhibit	professional
aware	demonstrate	exploit	media	role
coincide	dominate	generate	positive	

SELF-ASSESSMENT OF TARGET WORDS

Think carefully about how well you know each target word in this unit. Then, write it in the appropriate column in the chart.

I have never seen the word before.	I have seen the word but am not sure what it means.	I understand the word when I see or hear it in a sentence.	I have tried to use this word, but I am not sure I am using it correctly.	I use the word with confidence in either speaking *or* writing.	I use the word with confidence, both in speaking *and* writing.

BEFORE YOU READ

Read these questions. Discuss your answers in a small group.

1. How would you define success?

2. Are all famous people successful? Are all successful people famous? Give examples to support your opinion.

3. Name some people you consider successful. Why do you consider them successful?

READ

This article is an introduction to a book of advice about how to be successful. It defines success and explains what it takes to achieve it.

What Is Success?

What is success? Is it wealth? Fame? Power? We tend to think of success as something unusual, something that requires special talents to achieve. That's because stories in the
5 **media** about successful business executives, **professional** golfers, glamorous movie stars, best-selling authors, and powerful politicians lead us to believe that only a few special people are successful. We may not hear about them, but
10 ordinary people can be successful, too. Success is about reaching for something—and getting it. It is about having something you didn't have before. It is about **attaining** something that is valued by others.

15 Success begins with a clear goal, and attaining that goal requires ambition. Ambition is the energy that drives people to work hard, to learn more, and to seek opportunities to advance themselves. Some people have a clear goal, but
20 they lack the ambition to make their dream come true. Other people have great ambition but no clear goal to work toward. They start one scheme after another but never seem to find success.

25 All children begin life with great ambition. Consider the ambition that babies **demonstrate** as they try to sit up, crawl, and walk. Despite repeated failures, they keep trying until they succeed. What makes them keep trying?
30 Persistence. This is the ability to focus on a task despite interruptions, obstacles, and setbacks. Persistence is strong throughout childhood. During the teen years, however, a fear of failure or a fear of being laughed at by others for trying
35 to "be somebody" may **inhibit**, or stop, their persistence. As a result, many teens seem to just quit trying.

If parents are **aware** that a lack of ambition is common in teenagers, they may be able to
40 minimize it by providing **positive** learning experiences in the early years. For example, parents can encourage their young children to take on challenges, praise them for trying, and comfort them if they fail. One of the strongest
45 influences on a person's ambition is the family. It is not a **coincidence** that successful parents tend to raise successful children. However, is this due to heredity or upbringing? Evidence suggests that both play a **role** in determining
50 ambition.

The economic status of a family also influences a person's level of ambition. Young adults who grew up in poor families may be more focused on meeting the needs of
55 today rather than reaching for the dreams of tomorrow. Or they may have great ambition but lack the means to reach their goals. In contrast, ambition may be unnecessary for

those who grew up in rich families because, at least financially, they are already successful. Not surprisingly, ambition seems to coincide most often with middle-class status. Although financially secure, middle-class families may not feel socially secure. This status anxiety fuels the ambition needed to reach for success.

Despite their backgrounds, it is people with **dynamic** personalities who are most likely to succeed. These are people who don't wait for things to happen; these are people who take effective action to <u>make</u> things happen. With their eyes on the future, their goals **dominate** the choices they make. They learn the skills they will need through education or training. They **exploit**, that is, take advantage of, opportunities to broaden their knowledge through experience and observation. They seek assistance from anyone who might further their chances to succeed, including family members, friends, coaches, and **colleagues**.

And finally—with perhaps a bit of luck—success will come for these dynamic people. For each person it will be different, though, because individuals **generate** their own definitions of success. So he or she will get the job, win the race, earn the diploma, start the business, or climb the mountain—and the goal will be a reality.

READING COMPREHENSION

A. Mark each sentence as *T* (True) or *F* (False) according to the information in Reading 1. Use your dictionary to check the meaning of new words.

.... **1.** Stories generated by the media demonstrate that ordinary people can be successful.

.... **2.** Family plays a major role in influencing a child's level of ambition.

.... **3.** The teen years often coincide with a fear of failure and a lack of ambition.

.... **4.** Positive learning experiences in the early years can inhibit persistence.

.... **5.** Dynamic people are aware that they must take effective action to attain success.

.... **6.** Despite their backgrounds, professional people are the most likely to succeed.

.... **7.** Meeting the needs of today may dominate the thoughts of a young adult who grew up in a poor family.

.... **8.** People seeking success might ask colleagues to assist them.

.... **9.** One way to prepare for success is to exploit opportunities to learn through observation.

B. Put a check (✓) next to the qualities that contribute to success, according to Reading 1. Discuss your answers with a partner.

.... a clear goal   .... middle-class status   .... repeated failures

.... persistence   .... focus   .... a dynamic personality

.... a bit of luck   .... dreams of tomorrow   .... successful parents

READING STRATEGY: Identifying Definitions

> The author of Reading 1 uses the entire article to arrive at a full description
> of success. Each paragraph contains information that adds to the definition.
> Within the text, there are definitions of other words related to success.
> For some words, the author provides a definition, for example, *ambition* in
> paragraph 2. Other words are defined with a synonym, for example, *inhibit* in
> paragraph 3.

Look back at Reading 1 to find definitions of these words. Write the definitions in your notebook.

1. ambition (paragraph 2)

2. persistence (paragraph 3)

3. inhibit (paragraph 3)

4. dynamic people (paragraph 6)

5. exploit (paragraph 6)

STEP I VOCABULARY ACTIVITIES: Word Level

A. Use the target vocabulary in the box to complete this story. The words in parentheses can help you.

attained	dominant	positive
coincided with	dynamic	professional
demonstrated	generating	was aware

As a boy, Lance Armstrong excelled in many sports. By his teen years, however,
bicycling had become the .... interest in his life. He easily won many
 (1. most important)
local cycling races. But his goal was to be a .... racer. In his first race,
 (2. paid)
he finished last of 111 riders. He was discouraged and almost quit racing. Instead, he
trained harder and soon .... the rank of number one bicyclist in the
 (3. reached)
world. But his success .... a terrible illness. Lance, just 25 years old,
 (4. happened at the same time as)
was diagnosed with advanced cancer. After long and painful medical treatments, he
was so weak that he again thought of quitting. He .... that he might
 (5. knew)
never recover from his illness, but once more this .... young man
 (6. energetic)
.... amazing persistence, and he had a .... attitude.
 (7. showed) *(8. optimistic)*
He trained for two years, slowly regaining strength and .... a new
 (9. creating)
goal: to compete in the Tour de France bicycle race, one of the most demanding
sports contests in the world. In 1999, Lance entered the Tour and won. He
subsequently went on to win the Tour seven years in a row.

B. A *colleague* is a co-worker, someone you work with. Match the worker in the left column with his or her colleague on the right. Compare answers with a partner.

.... **1.** doctor   **a.** waiter

.... **2.** teacher   **b.** principal

.... **3.** manicurist   **c.** publisher

.... **4.** violinist   **d.** nurse

.... **5.** chef   **e.** pianist

.... **6.** author   **f.** hair stylist

In this unit, the word *role* is used to mean "the position or importance of something."

*Parents play a key **role** in the education of their children.*

*Exercise plays a **role** in staying healthy. Diet plays a **role**, too.*

Role is also commonly used to refer to the part of a character in a film or play.

*Several actors have played the **role** of Superman in films.*

C. According to Reading 1, which of these factors play a role when teenagers quit trying to succeed? Put a check (✓) next to these items.

.... fear of challenge   .... fear of being laughed at

.... lack of persistence   .... lack of setbacks

.... fear of failure   .... lack of experience

Now, with a partner, think of at least two other factors that may play a role. Discuss your ideas in a small group.

The *media* refers to the means of communication that reach many people, such as television, radio, and newspapers. *Media* is a plural noun. The singular form is *medium*, but this form is used less often. *Media* can also be used as an adjective.

*The news **media** cover national elections closely.*

*National elections get a lot of **media** coverage.*

*Some actors think that theater is a more satisfying **medium** than television.*

D. With a partner, describe these examples of media. Write *N* for news media, *P* for print media, and *A* for advertising media. More than one answer for each item is possible.

.... books   .... magazines   .... radio

.... the Internet   .... newspapers   .... television

E. To *generate* something means "to create, cause, or produce it." What do these workers generate? Complete the sentences. Then, add one more sentence of your own about another worker. Compare answers with a partner.

   1. A comedian generates .... in people who hear his jokes.

   2. A saleswoman generates .... for her company.

   3. A computer programmer generates .... for computers.

   4. An architect generates .... for new buildings.

   5. ....

STEP II VOCABULARY ACTIVITIES: Sentence Level

> The verb *coincide* means "to happen at the same time as another event." It can also be used to refer to two ideas or opinions that agree.
>
> *The release of Disney's new film was scheduled to **coincide** with the first day of vacation.*
>
> *Voters could not re-elect a mayor whose views did not **coincide** with theirs.*
>
> The noun form is *coincidence*. It refers to the surprising fact of two or more similar things happening at the same time by chance. The adjective form is *coincidental*.
>
> *By **coincidence**, June and Betty came to the party wearing identical outfits.*
>
> *It was a **coincidence** that they both wore the same outfit.*
>
> *It was also **coincidental** that their husbands were wearing matching shirts.*

F. For each of these sets of sentences, circle the one sentence that describes a coincidence. Then, write a sentence in your notebook explaining what the coincidence is, using the word *coincidence* or *coincidental*.

   1. a. Mr. Smith had spaghetti for lunch. His wife made spaghetti for dinner.
      b. Mr. and Mrs. Smith had spaghetti for dinner.

      By coincidence, Mr. Smith had spaghetti for lunch on the same day that his wife made spaghetti for dinner.

   2. a. Sam got on a bus to go downtown. His friend Judith was on the same bus.
      b. Ellen and Don got on a bus and they both went downtown to go to work.

   3. a. Mary and Larry are twins. Their birthdays are on March 1.
      b. Sue and Lou are neighbors. Their birthdays are on June 1.

   4. a. A family has five children. Each child's last name is Brown.
      b. A basketball team has five players. Each player's last name is Brown.

Word Form Chart

Noun	Verb	Adjective	Adverb
dominance domination	dominate	dominant	....

The verb *dominate* means "to have strong control over something" or "to be the most important part of something."

*My father **dominated** our lives when my brother and I were small.*

*The huge brick fireplace **dominated** the living room.*

G. Complete this paragraph, using different forms of *dominate*. Compare work with a partner.

The term "alpha male" is used in the science of animal behavior. It refers to the
(1) .... male in a group of animals, such as wolves. Among humans,
the alpha male tries to (2) .... all of the other males in his social
group, for example, his colleagues in the workplace. In the animal world, males may
fight to attain (3) .... over others. A human male may also "fight,"
but with words and actions that prove he is superior. Often the male who
(4) .... others is friendly and has clear goals, so others like having
him as their leader.

To be *aware* means "to know about or realize something." The noun form is
awareness. The antonym is *unaware*.

*Jon was **aware** that everyone was watching him.*

*Jon had no **awareness** that his name was called.*

*Jon was **unaware** of the audience's applause.*

H. In your notebook, complete these sentences about successful people. Use your own ideas. Compare sentences with a partner.

1. A successful teacher is aware that . . .
2. During the race, marathon runners may be unaware that . . .
3. Someone who is applying for a job must be aware of . . .
4. To write a successful book, an author must have an awareness of . . .

BEFORE YOU READ

Discuss your answers to these questions in a small group.

1. What is your definition of personality?
2. Do you know people who constantly talk about themselves? Why do you think they do that?
3. What are some things that famous people do that you don't approve of?

READ

This excerpt from a psychology textbook discusses a personality disorder called narcissism and the characteristics of people with this disorder.

I Love Me

Narcissus was the name of a god in an ancient Greek story. According to the story, he was very much in love with his own good looks. He drowned in a pool of water when he leaned
5 over too far to admire his handsome reflection. There is a mental illness named for Narcissus. It is called "narcissistic personality disorder." People with this disorder have great love for themselves, and this coincides with a strong
10 need to be admired by others.

Narcissus admiring his own reflection

Most people who have a narcissistic personality are very ordinary people. However, they think of themselves as being very important and special. As a result, they
15 often try to exploit others. They expect other people to give them constant attention and to obey their commands. In a restaurant, for example, a narcissist might expect to be seated immediately. He might demand a better table,

20 a special salad, or a sharper knife. Narcissists demand attention from everyone, including their family, friends, colleagues, and even strangers.

On the other hand, narcissists can demonstrate great charm. They smile and
25 flirt. They gossip and tell jokes. They generate excitement with their lively chatter. They like to talk about themselves and often dominate the conversation with stories about their exploits. In these stories they tend to greatly exaggerate
30 their talents and personal achievements.

In fact, when narcissists describe their achievements, they are likely to be lying. Lying is typical behavior for a narcissist, who often tries to impress people with false claims about things
35 he owns or people he knows. He brags that his golf clubs are identical to the ones used by Tiger Woods. He claims to be friends with the mayor and the police chief and the bank president.

This kind of talk seems to reflect great
40 self-confidence and self-esteem. However, psychiatrists suggest that this behavior results not from self-love, but actually from fear of failure and the subsequent shame it would bring. Some say that narcissism results if parents do
45 not comfort young children when they have been disappointed or have failed at something. The children view this as punishment and try to avoid future failure. As a result, they never learn to deal with disappointment or failure.

Other therapists have a slightly different theory. They believe that a narcissistic personality arises when parents try to protect children from disappointment and failure by satisfying all of their demands. This generates in the children a lifelong pattern of expecting that they will always get what they want.

Narcissists do not see other people as human beings but rather as objects that have no feelings or needs of their own. A narcissist believes that the role of other people is to satisfy his needs and to admire him. For this reason, a narcissist seldom has truly close friends. Instead he surrounds himself with people he considers worthy of his greatness.

Oddly, the narcissistic traits that we find so annoying in ordinary people are the same traits that attract us to many entertainers and professional athletes. A recent study found that celebrities as a group are more narcissistic than other people. However, it is not fame that makes celebrities narcissistic; it is the other way around. They were first narcissistic and were then drawn to careers that would earn them admiration from others.

The applause of their fans is a positive message that they are loved and admired. But they may also exploit the media to get attention. For example, they wear show-off clothes and date gorgeous partners. They marry and divorce again and again. They buy expensive cars and drive too fast. Whatever they do, the media report it because the uninhibited behavior and dynamic personalities of the celebrities make them seem exciting.

All of us have some narcissism, and that's good. Self-love is what motivates people to nourish and protect their bodies, to improve their minds, to learn new skills, and to discover the world in which they live. It is what gives people the self-confidence to share a relationship with others and the ambition to reach for success. However, the self-love of those with a serious narcissistic behavior disorder is so excessive that it overshadows everything else in their lives.

READING COMPREHENSION

Mark each sentence *T*(True) or *F*(False) according to the information in Reading 2. Use your dictionary to help you understand new words.

.... 1. Narcissists demand attention from everyone, including colleagues and strangers.

.... 2. A narcissist might try to exploit people because he believes he is very important.

.... 3. A narcissist is aware of other people's failures and demonstrates great concern.

.... 4. Narcissists often lie about their achievements and dominate conversations with stories about themselves.

.... 5. Psychiatrists believe that narcissistic behavior coincides with self-esteem.

.... 6. Psychiatrists believe that parents play a role in generating narcissism in their children.

.... 7. Celebrities get attention from the media because their behavior makes them seem uninhibited.

.... 8. Professional athletes become narcissistic as a result of their careers.

READING STRATEGY

A. Complete these sentences to define the characteristics of a narcissist. Refer to Reading 2 for information.

1. They think of themselves as being ....
2. They are often ....
3. They try to ....
4. They demand .... from ....
5. They can demonstrate ....
6. They like to ....
7. They often dominate ....
8. They tend to exaggerate ....
9. .... is typical behavior.
10. They believe that the role of other people is ....
11. Their self-love overshadows ....

B. Write a definition of narcissism in your own words.

....

STEP I VOCABULARY ACTIVITIES: Word Level

In this unit, the adjective *professional* is used to describe activities for which participants are paid. *A professional* (noun) is someone who is paid for his or her work. The adverb form is *professionally*.

*College sports dominate TV time on Saturdays and **professional** sports on Sundays.*

*My father is a **professional** artist. I'm just an amateur.*

*Her real name is Mary Jones, but she's known **professionally** as Lucille Fontaine.*

A. Work with a partner. Write *P* for each activity that is done only by professionals. Write *A* for each activity that is done for fun, only by amateurs. Write *B* for each activity that could be done by both professionals and amateurs.

.... 1. fishing
.... 2. designing airplanes
.... 3. skiing
.... 4. playing basketball
.... 5. watching television
.... 6. exercising
.... 7. taking photographs
.... 8. cooking
.... 9. performing surgery

A *dynamic* person is someone who is effective and active. He or she is full of ideas and energy.

> **Dynamic** *people make good leaders.*

Dynamic can also be used to refer to a force or energy that causes change in people or events.

> *Computers have had a* **dynamic** *influence on international communication.*

B. With a partner, decide which of these jobs could best be done by a dynamic person. Put a check (✓) next to these jobs. Explain your choices.

.... farmer   .... mail carrier   .... salesperson

.... film actor   .... politician   .... teacher

.... gardener   .... receptionist   .... wedding planner

Now, with your partner, complete these sentences with the names of inventions that have had a dynamic influence. (More than one answer is possible.)

1. .... has/have a dynamic influence on the way people cook.
2. .... has/have a dynamic influence on overseas travel.
3. .... has/have a dynamic influence on preventing illness.

The central meaning of the adjective *positive* is "yes." It has many uses:

good, helpful, or useful	*The new law had a* **positive** *effect on the economy.*
	Thank you for your **positive** *suggestions.*
accepting or approving	*The audience had a* **positive** *reaction to the new play.*
hopeful	*A* **positive** *attitude is important if you want to reach your goals.*
certain or confident	*I'm* **positive** *that Cairo is the capital of Egypt.*
affirming	*The blood test was* **positive***. She's definitely pregnant.*

C. These sentences are from the readings in this unit. Which meaning does *positive* have in each sentence? Discuss your answers with a partner.

1. If parents are aware that a lack of ambition is common in teenagers, they may be able to minimize it by providing positive learning experiences in the early years. (Reading 1)

2. The applause of their fans is a positive message that they are loved and admired. (Reading 2)

To *attain* something means "to succeed in achieving a goal, usually after great effort." Be careful not to confuse this word with "obtain," which means "to get something."

*Dr. Arnet **attained** the rank of professor. Then, he obtained a new desk for his office.*

D. Complete these sentences, using *obtained* or *attained*.

1. Fran Brown .... a driver's license.

2. Edith Charles .... an Olympic gold medal.

3. Admiral White .... command of a naval ship.

4. Sam Rich .... tickets for tomorrow's basketball game.

Now, with your partner, decide which of these things are attainable by most people. Which are unattainable? Write *A* for attainable and *U* for unattainable. Discuss your answers in a small group.

.... a high school diploma   .... an Olympics gold medal

.... a journey to the moon   .... fluency in a second language

.... a Nobel prize   .... happiness

.... a well-paying job   .... the command of a naval ship

STEP II VOCABULARY ACTIVITIES: Sentence Level

The verb *exploit* has the general meaning of "*use*," but use can express two different ideas. It's important to understand which idea is being expressed in a particular sentence.

use something cleverly or productively	*A good student **exploits** every opportunity to read outside of class.*
use something unfairly or selfishly	*Some companies **exploit** workers by not paying them a fair salary.*

The noun form, *exploitation,* almost always has the second, negative meaning.

*The **exploitation** of workers is unfair.*

E. Work with a partner. Write *P* for the sentences that use *exploit* in a positive way. Write *N* for the sentences that use the word in a negative way.

.... 1. Some parents exploit their children by pushing them to perform in movies or TV shows.

.... 2. He exploited every chance to sharpen his writing skills.

.... 3. She exploited her friends by borrowing money every day.

.... 4. He exploited his musical talent by playing with a band.

In this unit, *demonstrate* is used to mean "to prove or show something." A *demonstrative* person shows his or her feelings very clearly.

*Her paintings **demonstrate** a great love of her country.*

*My little granddaughter is so **demonstrative.** She is always hugging me.*

Another common meaning is "to give directions about how something is done."

*My trainer **demonstrated** how to use the new exercise bicycle.*

To *demonstrate* is also often used to mean "to publicly show your support for or against a social or political cause."

*A group was **demonstrating** in front of city hall yesterday.*

*Fifty **demonstrators** took part in a **demonstration** against the war.*

F. Complete this paragraph, using different forms of *demonstrate*. Compare work with a partner.

Although most narcissists live ordinary lives, is not unusual for a narcissist to become the leader of a nation. What better way to .... his or her importance? And this has happened many times in history. These leaders .... their power by demanding absolute loyalty from their people. They may order punishment for anyone who has .... disloyalty. If people try to organize a public .... against the government, the leader may have them arrested.

To *inhibit* an action means "to stop it or to decrease it."

*Fear of failure **inhibited** him from participating in the race.*

*Antibiotics **inhibit** the growth of bacteria.*

The noun form, *inhibition,* refers to the feeling of embarrassment or fear that stops someone from speaking freely or acting freely. The adjectives forms are *inhibited* and *uninhibited*.

*Most actors don't mind acting silly because they are **uninhibited.** They have no **inhibitions**. Most other adults have a hard time acting silly. They are too **inhibited**.*

G. Read this story. Then, in your notebook, rewrite the sentences using different forms of *inhibit*. Be prepared to read your sentences aloud or discuss them in a small group.

1. Last year, Ahn went to the U.S. because the economic slowdown in his home country reduced his professional opportunities.
2. Adjusting to a new country was hard. He was too shy to make friends with his colleagues. He worried that his English was poor.

continued

3. He wanted to feel more free when he spoke, so Ahn decided to join an English class.

4. His teacher told the students, "Try to lose your shyness and negative feelings. It's okay to make mistakes."

5. The teacher understood why the students were embarrassed. He made them feel more comfortable, and soon the students were laughing and talking, learning English, and making friends.

H. Self-Assessment Review: Go back to page 57 and reassess your knowledge of the target vocabulary. How has your understanding of the words changed? What words do you feel most comfortable with now?

WRITING AND DISCUSSION TOPICS

1. Sir Winston Churchill said this about success: "Success is the ability to go from one failure to another with no loss of enthusiasm." Do you agree or disagree? Give an example to support your opinion.

2. Charles Luckman described success like this: "Success is that old ABC—ability, breaks, and courage." Do you agree or disagree? Give an example to support your opinion.

3. Imagine you are writing a letter to a company that you would like to work for as an automobile salesperson. What qualities are important for someone in this position? What would you say about yourself that would be truthful yet emphasize your positive qualities?

4. Describe someone you know (or someone you have read about) who is successful. What kind of person is he or she? What did he or she do to attain success?

5. Can a narcissistic person also be a successful person? What qualities do narcissistic people have that might help them be successful? What qualities might inhibit their success?

SOLVING CRIMES WITH SCIENCE

In this unit, you will

- ⊃ read about the use of science to solve crimes.
- ⊃ learn to identify time and sequence words.
- ⊃ increase your understanding of the target academic words for this unit:

authority	contrary	instance	panel	tape
conclude	detect	logic	site	technical
consult	establish	motive	specific	

SELF-ASSESSMENT OF TARGET WORDS

Think carefully about how well you know each target word in this unit. Then, write it in the appropriate column in the chart.

I have never seen the word before.	I have seen the word but am not sure what it means.	I understand the word when I see or hear it in a sentence.	I have tried to use this word, but I am not sure I am using it correctly.	I use the word with confidence in either speaking *or* writing.	I use the word with confidence, both in speaking *and* writing.

MORE WORDS YOU'LL NEED

detective: a person, usually a police officer, who helps solve crimes

evidence: signs or proof that something exists or is true

suspect: a person that police believe may have committed a crime

BEFORE YOU READ

Read these questions. Discuss your answers in a small group.

1. Do you ever watch crime stories on television? If so, which one is your favorite?
2. Why do you think people like movies, TV programs, or books about solving crimes?
3. What are some ways that science can help the police solve crimes?

READ

This newspaper article tells the story of how the police solved the case of a mysterious death.

Solving a Crime with Science: A True Story

On the morning of June 11, 1986, Sue Snow woke up with a headache. She took two Extra-Strength Excedrin capsules and within minutes she collapsed to the floor. She was rushed to a
5 hospital, but died hours later.

Doctors were unable to explain Sue's death. They asked the hospital laboratory to do some tests to **establish** the cause. One test **detected** cyanide, a poison that can rapidly kill a person
10 who swallows even a small amount. The hospital immediately called the police. They began their investigation by interviewing members of Sue's family.

Mrs. Snow's daughter recalled that her mother
15 had a headache the morning she died and that she had taken two Extra-Strength Excedrin capsules. When a police laboratory subsequently tested the capsules remaining in the Excedrin bottle, the capsules were found to contain
20 cyanide.

The police **consulted** the manufacturers of Excedrin. The drug company used its **authority** to have stores immediately remove all bottles of Extra-Strength Excedrin from their shelves.
25 The police crime laboratory tested capsules from these thousands of bottles and found two that also contained cyanide. These bottles came from stores in two nearby towns. Police visited the two **sites** but learned nothing. Through the
30 media, they warned people about the poisoned medicine and asked them to phone if they had any useful information.

Six days after Sue Snow's death, a woman named Stella Nickell phoned the police to
35 report that her husband, Bruce, had died suddenly on June 5 after taking Extra-Strength Excedrin capsules. When the police searched Stella Nickell's house, they found two bottles of poisoned Extra-Strength Excedrin capsules.
40 A police detective thought something was very odd. The crime laboratory had tested over 740,000 Extra-Strength Excedrin capsules and found poisoned capsules in only five bottles: two from sites in nearby towns, one in Sue
45 Snow's house and two in Stella Nickell's house. Mrs. Nickell claimed that she had bought her two bottles at two different stores on two different days. **Contrary** to what she claimed, the detective thought that it would be nearly
50 impossible for one person to coincidentally buy *two* of the five poisoned bottles.

Could Stella Nickell have poisoned the capsules that killed her husband and Sue Snow? It didn't seem likely. She was
55 a grandmother and worked as an airport security guard. Friends and family said that she and her husband seemed happy. Then detectives learned that Stella and her husband were deeply in debt. They also learned that

Bruce Nickell had a life insurance policy that would pay Stella $31,000 when he died, but would pay her $176,000 if his death were accidental.

The detectives knew that money can be a strong **motive** for murder. They **concluded** that Stella had put cyanide in five Excedrin bottles. She kept two and placed three others in nearby stores. Sue Snow bought one of those bottles. Stella probably hoped that a careless drug company or a crazed person would be blamed if people died from the poisoned capsules. Stella probably thought she had created a clever scheme to make her husband's death seem accidental so she could collect $176,000.

Although the detectives felt certain that Stella had poisoned the Excedrin, **technically** they were unable to link her to the poison. They wondered how she had learned about cyanide. At a public library near Stella's house, a librarian told detectives that Stella had borrowed several books about poison. One was named *Human Poisoning*. A crime laboratory examined these books and found 84 **instances** of Stella's fingerprints, most of them on pages about cyanide.

When confronted with the **specific** evidence against her, Stella admitted that she had put poison in the Excedrin capsules. A jury **panel** found her guilty of murder, and a judge sentenced her to 99 years in prison. **Logical** thinking, persistent detective work, and science worked together to help the police solve the crime.

READING COMPREHENSION

Mark each sentence as *T* (True) or *F* (False) according to the information in Reading 1. Use your dictionary to check the meaning of new words.

.... **1.** Doctors in the hospital established that Sue Snow died of a headache.

.... **2.** A laboratory detected cyanide in a bottle of Excedrin found at Sue Snow's house.

.... **3.** The police consulted with the drug company to find out which stores were selling Excedrin.

.... **4.** The drug company used its authority to close the stores where Excedrin was sold.

.... **5.** Instances of poisoned bottles of Excedrin were found at five sites.

.... **6.** Contrary to what Stella claimed, it would have been possible for her to buy two poisoned bottles of Excedrin coincidentally.

.... **7.** The police concluded that Stella's motive for poisoning the Excedrin was to get $176,000 from her husband's insurance policy.

.... **8.** The police believed that Stella had poisoned the Excedrin but they were technically not able to link her to the cyanide.

.... **9.** One specific book, named *Human Poisoning*, had Stella's fingerprints on 84 pages.

.... **10.** A combination of science, logical thinking, and good luck helped the police solve the crime.

READING STRATEGY: Identifying Time and Sequence Words

Understanding the *order of events* in a story is often essential for understanding the story, especially a mystery such as Reading 1. The order of events can be shown in several ways:

1. Sentences in a paragraph usually describe actions in the order that they happened.

2. Time words such as *Monday, March, summer*, or *1987* tell when actions took place.

3. Words such as *before, after, soon, first, next, meanwhile, then, finally*, and *subsequently* can show the order of events.

4. Phrases such as *three days later, the next year*, and *at the same time* also show time order.

A. Use time clues in the reading to determine the date of each of these events.

Sue Snow died ....

Bruce Nickell died ....

Stella Nickell phoned the police ....

B. A mystery story often presents events in the order that detectives learn about them. The reader has to figure out the real order of events. What is the likely sequence in which these events happened? Number them in order from 1 to 5.

.... Stella created a clever scheme.

.... Stella borrowed library books about poisons.

.... Stella poisoned 5 bottles of Extra-Strength Excedrin.

.... Sue Snow bought a bottle of Extra-Strength Excedrin.

.... Stella placed 3 bottles of Extra-Strength Excedrin in nearby stores.

STEP I VOCABULARY ACTIVITIES: Word Level

The verb *consult* means "to ask somebody for information" or "to seek information in a book or other reference."

*The police **consulted** a doctor to learn about the effects of the drug.*

*I **consulted** my calendar to see when my dentist appointment was.*

A. With a partner, decide whom or what you would consult for information about each of these things.

1. the meaning of a word

2. the telephone number of a restaurant

3. the price of an airplane ticket to London

4. a recipe for chicken soup

B. Use the target vocabulary in the box to complete this story. The words in parentheses can help you.

conclude	detect	logic
consult	establish	site
contrary	instance	specific

Sherlock Holmes is a fictional detective, created by Sir Arthur Conan Doyle about a hundred years ago. Readers learn that Holmes is known for using

.... and observation to solve crimes. As a result, the police
   (1. *reasoning*)

.... him when they have a difficult case. In each .... ,
   (2. *ask advice from*)   (3. *event*)

Holmes carefully examines the crime .... for evidence. He might
                                               (4. *location*)

.... faint footprints that the police overlooked. He might find a
   (5. *notice*)

broken clock that can .... the .... time the crime
                            (6. *tell*)   (7. *exact*)

was committed. He often discusses the evidence with his friend, Dr. Watson. Usually

Watson reasons incorrectly. He might say, "Then I must .... that
                                               (8. *decide*)

the husband did it." "On the .... , my dear Watson," Holmes might
                             (9. *opposite*)

reply. "It was her jealous sister."

A *site* is a location or a place where an event has happened or will happen.

   *Police were called to the **site** of the accident.*

A *website* is a location on the Internet.

   *The university's **website** listed all of the faculty members.*

C. Match the sites on the left with the people who might go to that site on the right. Then, tell a partner the reasons why the people go to the sites.

.... 1. accident site   **a.** a rock band

.... 2. construction site   **b.** a bride and groom

.... 3. battle site   **c.** emergency medical team

.... 4. wedding site   **d.** students

.... 5. concert site   **e.** carpenters

.... 6. graduation site   **f.** soldiers

A *motive* is a reason for an action. The word is often used, as it is in this unit, to refer to the reason someone commits a crime.

Jim needed money fast. That was his **motive** *for robbing the store.*

There are other, equally common usages of *motive* and its forms. The verb *motivate* means "to cause someone to act in a particular way," or "to make someone want to do something."

Desire to attend the music academy **motivated** *her to practice every day.*

The promise of a raise can **motivate** *employees to work harder.*

The noun form is *motivation*. It refers to the reason for doing something, or a positive feeling about doing something.

The employees showed a lot of **motivation** *and finished the project quickly.*

Someone who feels eager to do something is *motivated*. Someone who does not feel eager to do something is *unmotivated*.

Despite interesting lessons and good teachers, some kids remain **unmotivated.**

D. Write sentences in your notebook, according to the directions. Discuss your sentences in a small group.

1. Teachers are often motivating influences on their students. Write two sentences about other people who might also motivate a person to act.

2. Write one sentence describing a time when you were motivated to do something. What or who motivated you? How?

3. Write one sentence telling why you think some children are unmotivated in school.

Establish is commonly used to mean "to start something," like "establish a new school." In the context of this unit, however, *establish* is used to mean "to learn facts that prove something is true."

Detectives **established** *that the murdered man owed money to many people.*

E. Write the answers to these questions in your notebook. Refer to Reading 1 for information. Write complete sentences, using a form of *establish* in each.

1. What did the hospital laboratory find out about Sue's death? (Paragraph 2)

2. What did the police learn about the two nearby towns? (Paragraph 4)

3. What did the detectives find out about Bruce Nickell's insurance? (Paragraph 7)

4. What did the detectives learn at the public library? (Paragraph 9)

The adjective *specific* means "detailed" or "exact." It can also be used to refer to something particular rather than general. The adverb form is *specifically*. The verb form is *specify*. *Specifics* is a noun that means "facts" or "details."

F. Read these sentences about what the police do after a crime has occurred. Rewrite the sentences in your notebook, using the form of *specific* in parentheses.

1. The police ask many definite questions, like the victim's name and age. (*specific*)
2. They need to know what happened. (*specifics*)
3. They want to know the details about when the crime happened. (*specifically*)
4. They want witnesses to tell exactly what they saw. (*specify*)
5. They hope witnesses can give them particular information about the crime. (*specific*)

The noun *logic* refers to the use of reasoning to decide if something is possible or correct.

> Instead of using **logic** to solve the puzzle, he tried guessing.

A *logical* decision or idea is reasonable and sensible. A decision that is based on guessing, feelings, or unreasonable conclusions is *illogical*.

> It did not seem **logical** that a man would buy a car and then sell it the next day.
>
> It seemed **illogical** for him to buy a car one day and sell it the next.

G. Read this story. Then, in your notebook, write five sentences about the facts in the story. Use forms of *establish*, *logical*, and *motive*. Be prepared to read aloud or discuss your sentences in a small group.

Mr. Able, a jewelry store owner, claims he was robbed of $1 million in jewels. He sued his insurance company when the company refused to pay him for the loss. Mr. Able said that one rainy winter day, a robber ran into the store carrying a gun and an umbrella. The robber kept the gun pointed at Mr. Able as he tied up his hands. Then the robber opened the safe in the back room and took all 536 pieces of jewelry. He stuffed them into a suitcase and ran out the door.

The insurance company's lawyer had a contrary point of view. He concluded that the details of Mr. Able's story are technically impossible. The lawyer said that the tape in the store's surveillance camera would show what really happened and prove that Mr. Able was lying. The tape shows the robber entering the store wearing a raincoat and carrying an umbrella—but they are not wet. He is not carrying a suitcase. The tape shows Mr. Able helping the robber tie his hands. The robber disappears into a back room for just 14 seconds, then leaves the store carrying a suitcase. The suitcase is too small to hold 536 pieces of jewelry. The robber leaves nearly $20,000 cash in the safe. The lawyer claimed that a friend pretended to rob Mr. Able for a share of the insurance money. His reason—he wanted to get rich quick.

BEFORE YOU READ

Read these questions. Discuss your answers in a small group.

1. What does a detective do?

2. How can a science laboratory be used to help solve a crime?

3. Is it possible for someone to commit a "perfect" crime that leaves no clues? Why or why not?

READ

This article discusses the role of scientific laboratory analysis in helping the police solve crimes.

Forensic Science

Sherlock Holmes, a fictional detective of a century ago, was one of the first to use forensic science—the scientific analysis of physical evidence to solve crimes. Holding
5 a big magnifying glass, Holmes inspected crime scenes for footprints, broken glass, hair—anything that might help identify the person who committed the crime. In today's world, Holmes might be a CSI, or crime scene
10 investigator.

Sherlock Holmes, from the Arthur Conan Doyle stories

Today, when a crime is reported, a murder for instance, the police immediately send a medical examiner (ME) and a CSI team to the crime site. The ME and CSIs will be part of a panel of
15 technical experts in the investigation.

At the crime scene, the ME examines the body of the victim and looks for wounds or marks that might be related to the crime. The ME also takes many photographs of the body.
20 The body is subsequently taken away for a detailed examination that will establish the cause and time of the victim's death.

Meanwhile, CSIs first take hundreds of photographs of the crime site. Next they check
25 the site for fingerprints. Most fingerprints form when sweat or another oily substance on a fingertip leaves an invisible imprint on a glass, tabletop, or other object. CSIs dust a black powder on objects at the crime site to
30 make these prints visible. The CSIs then look for drops of blood, strands of hair, pieces of ripped cloth, or other evidence that might link someone to the crime site.

"Every contact leaves a trace," according to an
35 authority in forensics. This means that whenever a crime involves physical contact, the criminal either leaves something at the site, takes something from the site, or both. This might be any number of substances, including hair, animal
40 fur, sand, grass, and fibers from clothing or carpeting. Such trace evidence is usually difficult to detect, so, like Sherlock Holmes, CSIs rely on handheld magnifying glasses to examine the crime scene. CSIs might even vacuum the entire
45 area to collect tiny samples. They carefully label each piece of evidence as they collect it.

The collected evidence is then sent to a forensics laboratory. There, forensic scientists will analyze it to establish how and when the murder took place, where it took place, and who did it. Sometimes the evidence will even show *why* it took place, that is, the motive for the killing.

Among all the evidence found at the site, fingerprints are conclusive in linking a specific person to the crime scene. This is because no two people have the same fingerprints. Fingerprints from a crime scene are analyzed by computer to determine if they match the prints of a known criminal or crime suspect.

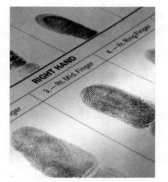

Fingerprints are vital evidence.

DNA is another conclusive means of identification because each person's DNA is unique. DNA is contained in cells of the body, so that evidence of hair, blood, tears, sweat, or other bodily fluids found at a crime scene can be used to link a specific person to the crime. Like fingerprints, DNA samples are analyzed by computer to determine if they match the DNA of a known criminal or a suspect.

Voices, too, are unique. Samples of voices from security camera **tapes**, telephone answering machines, or other recording devices can be scanned electronically. A printout of the scan will show patterns of highs and lows, rhythm, and volume that can be compared to patterns of a suspect's voice. However, authorities have contrary opinions about using voiceprints for identification. Some argue that voices can change over time as people age or suffer illnesses, so old voiceprints are not always reliable.

In the laboratory, forensic scientists use an electron microscope to scan samples of the substances that were collected at the crime scene. Then they enlarge the samples (up to 150,000×) on a visual display unit. This allows them to easily compare those samples with samples found at another location or on a suspect's clothing.

Forensic laboratories have on file the shoe print patterns of thousands of kinds of shoes. These can be compared to shoeprints found at a crime scene to establish the size and kind of shoes worn by a suspect. If the shoeprint was made in a soft material, like mud, the lab may be able to tell the height and weight of the person by the depth of each step and the distance between steps.

After all of the evidence has been analyzed, the police chief consults with panel members. Based on the evidence, they determine if it is logical to accuse and arrest a crime suspect. If it is, members of the panel may later be asked to present their forensic evidence in a court of law as proof of a suspect's guilt.

READING COMPREHENSION

Mark each sentence as *T* (True) or *F* (False) according to the information in Reading 2. Use your dictionary to check the meaning of new words.

.... 1. Holmes inspected a crime site for anything related to the crime, for instance footprints, broken glass, or hair.

.... 2. CSIs are part of a panel of technical experts in a forensic investigation.

.... 3. Forensic laboratories establish when and where a murder took place by taking hundreds of photographs.

.... 4. To identify footprints, forensic laboratories consult files of footprints of known criminals.

.... 5. CSIs use handheld magnifying glasses to detect trace evidence at crime scenes.

.... 6. Authorities have contrary opinions about using fingerprints for identification.

.... 7. DNA analysis can conclusively establish the motive for a crime.

.... 8. Samples of a suspect's voice can be compared to voice samples from surveillance tapes or telephone answering machines.

.... 9. A suspect will be arrested if, based on the evidence, it seems logical that he or she committed the crime.

.... 10. Fingerprints found at a crime scene can be linked to a specific individual if they match the individual's fingerprints.

READING STRATEGY

A. Reread the first four paragraphs of Reading 2. Then, write the time word or phrase that answers these questions.

1. When did Sherlock Holmes do his detective work? ....

2. When do the police send an ME and a CSI team? ....

3. When do the CSIs take photographs in relation to other tasks? ....

B. Number these tasks, from *1* to *7*, in the order in which they are done by the CSI team.

.... dust objects for fingerprints

.... take photographs

.... send evidence to a forensics laboratory

.... present their evidence in a court of law

.... look for drops of blood or strands of hair

.... label the evidence

.... consult with the police chief

STEP I VOCABULARY ACTIVITIES: Word Level

The adjective *technical* refers to the knowledge of machines, materials, and processes used in science and industry.

> *Forensic scientists use their **technical** skills to analyze crime scene evidence.*

This unit also uses the adverb *technically,* which means "to show an exact interpretation of a law or a fact."

> *You can't come in yet. It's only 9:58. **Technically,** the store doesn't open until 10:00.*

Another common use of the word *technical* is to refer to words and concepts related to a particular subject.

> *"Stress" is a **technical** word used in engineering.*

A. Complete the story with the words from the box.

technical assistance	technical person
technical explanation	technical words

My computer printer wasn't working right, so I called the company hotline for (1) .... The guy on the phone gave me a (2) .... of the problem. I said, "Stop! You're using too many (3) .... I'm not a (4) ...."

So he said, "See the button that says ON? Just push that."

B. With a partner, complete these sentences with your own ideas. Share your ideas with the class.

1. "I know your 21st birthday is tomorrow, but today you are technically . . ."
2. "The sign says 3 lemons for $1. Technically, one lemon would cost . . ."
3. "Waiter, a fly fell into my soup."
   "I'm sorry, but the restaurant is not technically responsible for . . ."
4. "I see the sign that says No Parking, but technically I'm not parked, I'm just . . ."

C. With a partner, decide who has the authority to punish someone who breaks the rules or laws in these situations.

1. in a soccer game   3. in a city   5. in an office
2. in a classroom   4. in a family   6. in a store

An *authority* is a recognized expert in a field. The adjective form is *authoritative*.

> *Professor West is an **authority** on the history of crime.*
> *He wrote an **authoritative** book titled Crime in Nineteenth Century Britain.*

An *authority* is also a person or group that has the power to make rules or laws.

> *The city transportation **authority** wants the bus company to add new routes.*

Authority (noncount noun) refers to the power that such a person or group has.

> *Parental **authority** today is not as strong as it was in the past.*

D. Match the authorities on the left with their fields of expertise on the right. Then, tell a partner how the two ideas are connected.

.... **1.** a professor of 16th-century French literature   **a.** Computer Science Department

.... **2.** a professor of contemporary painting   **b.** Foreign Language Department

.... **3.** a professor of rocket science   **c.** Art Department

.... **4.** a professor of cybertechnology   **d.** Engineering Department

STEP II VOCABULARY ACTIVITIES: Sentence Level

Word Form Chart			
Noun	Verb	Adjective	Adverb
detective detection detector	detect	detectable	....

E. Complete this paragraph by using a form of *detect* in each blank. Compare work with a partner.

A polygraph is a machine that is often called a "lie (1) ...."
It is used by some (2) .... when they question suspects. The
polygraph is based on the belief that, if a person is lying, his body will react with
(3) .... physical changes, such as increased blood pressure and heart
rate. The machine (4) .... these changes and records them. If the
polygraph shows that physical changes occurred when the suspect answered, the
(5) .... concludes that the suspect is lying. However, polygraph tests
are only 70–90% accurate. This means that 10–30% of those tested might escape
(6) .... even if they are guilty—or they might be considered guilty
even though they are innocent.

An *instance* is an example or case of a particular kind of occurrence.

*Yesterday's bank robbery was another **instance** of crime in the neighborhood.*

For instance is a common phrase that means, "for example."

*Bank security was poor. **For instance**, the cashiers had no warning alarms.*

F. Match each sentence on the right with the example that goes with it on the left. Use *for instance* to join the sentences, and write them in your notebook. Compare answers with a partner.

> *Bank security was poor. For instance, there was no guard at the door.*

_e_ **1.** Bank security was poor.   **a.** the note said GIV ME YOR MONEE.

.... **2.** The robbers were armed.   **b.** none had a specific job to do.

.... **3.** The robbers didn't plan very well.   **c.** each robber had a gun or a knife.

.... **4.** The robbers covered their faces.   **d.** one was wearing a black ski mask.

.... **5.** The robbers did not seem very smart.   **e.** there was no guard at the door.

The verb *conclude* has the general meaning of "end" or "finish." It can also mean "to reach a decision after thought or study." The adjective *conclusive* refer to something that is definitely true.

*The lawyer **concluded** his summation of the case and calmly sat down.*

*The jury **concluded** that the suspect was guilty.*

*His fingerprint on the knife is **conclusive** proof that he is guilty.*

The noun form is *conclusion*. It is used in some common expressions:

reach a conclusion	make a judgment after careful consideration
come to a conclusion	make a decision after careful consideration
jump to conclusions	make a judgment based on feelings, not facts

G. Read these statements about a crime. Then, answer each question that follows, using a form of *conclude*. Be prepared to read aloud and explain your answers in a small group.

- A valuable painting was stolen from a popular art museum.
- Jim's fingerprints were found on the wall where the painting had been.
- Jim said he didn't steal the painting. A polygraph test showed that he was not lying.
- His girlfriend, Linda, says that Jim was with her at the time the theft took place.
- The painting was found in Linda's house. It had Linda's fingerprints on it.

1. Who did the police decide was guilty?

2. What did the police decide about the fingerprints on the wall? Why?

3. What evidence proved who was guilty?

H. Read this story. Then, in your notebook, rewrite the story in your own words. Use *detect*, *detective*, *consult*, *consultant*, and *consultation* in your version. Be prepared to present your work in class.

One day, a man disappeared from his office. His family, friends, and colleagues couldn't supply any useful information. No one noticed anything unusual about the man's office, and there was no crime scene to search for evidence. In this case, the police decided to seek the advice of a psychic—a person who claims to have special powers, such as seeing the future or hearing messages from dead people. The police went to the psychic's office for a meeting. She asked to hold the missing man's hairbrush so that she could try to "see" him and "hear" him talk. Who knows what the psychic will discover? There is no scientific proof of psychic powers, but sometimes this kind of information can give the police investigation a new direction, and missing people can be found.

I. Self-Assessment Review: Go back to page 71 and reassess your knowledge of the target vocabulary. How has your understanding of the words changed? What words do you feel most comfortable with now?

WRITING AND DISCUSSION TOPICS

1. Find an article in a newspaper or news magazine that describes a crime. Describe what happened, using as many target words from this unit as possible.

2. The Facial Action Coding System is a system that allows trained users to detect lying by looking at the facial expressions of a crime suspect. The system identifies 46 facial movements that suggest either honesty or deception. Does this system seem like a useful one for the police? What might be some advantages and disadvantages of such a system?

3. What qualities should a good police detective have? Why?

4. How have computers helped the police solve crimes? Give some examples. You can do some research on the Internet to find information.

5. Before forensic science became the standard way to solve crimes, police often depended on motive and opportunity as indications of guilt. That is, if someone had a reason to commit the crime, and they had the chance to do it, then they were considered guilty. Do you think this method is fair or unfair? Explain your opinion.

6. In some countries, the media are given access to information about crimes as details become available. In other countries, the media may not publish or broadcast information about a crime investigation. Which do you think is the better way? Why?

THE FAST-FOOD REVOLUTION

In this unit, you will

- ➲ read about the fast food revolution and the subsequent expansion of franchises.
- ➲ learn how to read numerical tables.
- ➲ increase your understanding of the target academic words for this unit:

abandon	complement	decade	generation	output
acknowledge	contemporary	economy	grade	overlap
albeit	contrast	expand	incline	reject

SELF-ASSESSMENT OF TARGET WORDS

Think carefully about how well you know each target word in this unit. Then, write it in the appropriate column in the chart.

I have never seen the word before.	I have seen the word but am not sure what it means.	I understand the word when I see or hear it in a sentence.	I have tried to use this word, but I am not sure I am using it correctly.	I use the word with confidence in either speaking *or* writing.	I use the word with confidence, both in speaking *and* writing.

MORE WORDS YOU'LL NEED

chain: a group of stores, in different locations, that are owned by the same person or corporation

retail business: a business that sells goods or services directly to customers, such as grocery stores, car dealers, and barber shops

BEFORE YOU READ

Read these questions. Discuss your answers in a small group.

1. Think about the last time you ate in a fast-food restaurant. What did you eat? Besides the food, name three good things about your experience.

2. Why do some people dislike fast-food restaurants? Do you agree with their complaints?

3. Why do you think there are so many fast-food restaurants?

READ

This article discusses the many reasons behind the worldwide expansion of fast-food restaurants.

The Fast-Food Revolution

Maurice and Richard McDonald made a lot of money with their restaurant, but they grew tired of the stresses of ownership. The brothers were tired of searching for replacements when their cooks and waitresses quit. They were tired of replacing broken dishes and glassware and lost silverware. Before **abandoning** their successful business, however, they decided to try a new system of preparing and serving food.

Their remodeled restaurant **contrasted** with the original. It served just hamburgers, cheeseburgers, French fries, and drinks. Paper wrappers and paper cups replaced the dishes and glassware. Silverware wasn't needed because the restaurant didn't serve any food that required a knife, fork, or spoon to eat. Gone also were the professional cooks. Instead, food preparation was divided among several workers, each with a specific task. One worker grilled the hamburgers; another wrapped them in paper; a third cooked French fries; and another poured drinks. There were no waitresses. Customers ordered and paid at the counter then carried their own food to a table. This new system was like a factory assembly line. Increasing the speed of food preparation increased the kitchen's **output** and lowered its costs. The system revolutionized the restaurant business and introduced the term "fast food."

Carl Karcher heard that a nearby restaurant was selling cheap, **albeit** top-**grade**, hamburgers for 15 cents. He was charging 35 cents for burgers in his own restaurant. When he visited the McDonald's restaurant, he was astonished to see dozens of customers waiting in line to buy burgers while the assembly-line kitchen staff quickly and efficiently prepared their food. He liked the new system. In 1956 Karcher opened his own fast-food restaurant and named it Carl's Jr.

Around this time, Ray Kroc, a salesman who sold milkshake machines to restaurants, also visited the new McDonald's restaurant. Kroc was impressed by its food preparation and service system. He convinced the McDonald brothers to sell him the rights to build McDonald's restaurants across the U.S. By 1960, Kroc had opened 250 of them. A **decade** later, there were nearly 3,000 McDonald's franchises across the U.S.

McDonald's revolutionized the restaurant industry.

The fast food industry grew because it was born at the right time. In the 1950s, the **economy** of the U.S. was **expanding**, and people were **inclined** to be optimistic and ambitious. This was a **generation** that was willing to risk starting a business and to work hard to make it successful. They also trusted technology and **acknowledged** that machines could work as efficiently as individuals. Meanwhile, the automobile was growing in popularity, and this was, by far, the most important factor that led to the enormous growth of the fast-food industry.

New technology had made automobiles dependable and easy to drive. They were also affordable in the growing economy. People wanted to go places, and a national highway system, expanded during the 1950s, enabled U.S. families to drive long distances. They needed gas stations where they could refuel their vehicles and restaurants where they could eat. In time, hundreds of new gas stations were built along the highways, **complemented** by new fast-food restaurants where hungry travelers could get a quick meal.

The McDonald's model was widely copied in these restaurants, often by inexperienced owners who wanted a fast route to success. Some of the new restaurants failed, but many succeeded. Some even expanded into nationwide and worldwide chains. Among the **contemporary** start-ups of the 1950s and 1960s were Taco Bell, Burger King, Wendy's, Domino's Pizza, Kentucky Fried Chicken (KFC), and Jack in the Box.

The amazing success of fast-food chains soon inspired other kinds of retail businesses to form national and international chains of stores. Although many people **reject** the idea of globalization, business chains are rapidly **overlapping** national borders and spreading around the world.

READING COMPREHENSION

Mark each sentence as *T* (True) or *F* (False) according to the information in Reading 1. Use your dictionary to help you understand new words.

.... **1.** Maurice and Richard McDonald abandoned their restaurant because the output was low and it did not make enough money.

.... **2.** Their original restaurant used glassware. In contrast, the new restaurant used paper cups.

.... **3.** McDonald's hamburgers were top-grade but very expensive.

.... **4.** In the decade between 1960 and 1970, McDonald's expanded to around 3,000 restaurants nationwide.

.... **5.** Among the contemporary start-ups of the 1950s and 1960s were Domino's Pizza and Wendy's.

.... **6.** In the 1950s, people were optimistic, albeit inclined to worry about the economy.

.... **7.** This generation rejected fast foods because they acknowledged the new food preparation system was not efficient.

.... **8.** Many roadside stops included the complement of gas stations and fast-food restaurants.

.... **9.** Many business chains are overlapping U.S. borders into other countries.

READING STRATEGY: Reading Numerical Tables

> *Numerical tables* can provide a lot of information in a small space. The information is usually arranged in rows and columns, which makes it easy to read and to compare facts. To preview a table or chart:
>
> **1.** Read the title to see what kind of information is given.
>
> **2.** Read the labels at the top of each column.
>
> **3.** Note the date of the table so that you will know how recent the information is.

Read through the table. Then, use the information in this table to answer the questions below.

2005 Status of Fast-Food Restaurants That Started in the 1950s & 1960s		
Franchise	**Start-Up Year**	**Est. Number of Franchises**
Domino's Pizza	1960	7,320
Jack in the Box	1951	2,000
Taco Bell	1962	4,800
Wendy's	1969	6,600

1. Which of these fast-food restaurants was the first to open? Which of them opened most recently?

2. Which of these fast-food restaurants has the greatest number of franchises?

3. How many franchises did Domino's Pizza have in 2005?

STEP I VOCABULARY ACTIVITIES: Word Level

A. Use the target vocabulary in the box to complete this story. The words in parentheses can help you.

abandon	expand	inclined
acknowledges	generations	rejecting
albeit	in contrast	

The people of past .... ate in restaurants only on weekends or
(1. *people born at about the same time*)
special occasions. ...., people today are .... to eat
(2. *showing a difference*)   (3. *likely*)
out several times a week. This could be a problem if their menu choice is always a

hamburger and French fries. Nearly everyone .... that too much
(4. *agrees that it's true*)
fat in the diet is not healthy. Unfortunately, hamburgers and French fries are high

in fat, ... delicious. Instead of .... fast food
(5. *although*)   (6. *refusing*)
altogether, people should simply .... the burgers and fries and
(7. *stop having*)
.... their food choices by ordering something different.
(8. *increase*)

B. Write the length of each time period. Consult your dictionary, if needed.

1. a week   ...7... days   4. a millennium   .... years
2. a decade   .... years   5. leap year   .... days
3. a century   .... years

C. *Output* refers to the production of something or the amount of something produced. Match the output on the right with the person, machine, or business that produces it on the left. Then, tell a partner how the two ideas are connected.

.... 1. an automobile factory   a. stories
.... 2. a movie studio   b. milk
.... 3. a bakery   c. films
.... 4. an author   d. electricity
.... 5. a power plant   e. cakes and pies
.... 6. a dairy   f. new cars

A *generation* is the group of people (in a family or a society) who are approximately the same age.

Americans born in the late 1960s and 1970s are informally called "Generation X."

People who are approximately the same age are *contemporaries* (noun).

Your generation liked rock and roll. My contemporaries prefer hip hop.

The adjective *contemporary* is used to refer to things that happen or exist at about the same time.

The increase in cars in the U.S. was contemporary with the beginning of fast-food restaurants.

Another common use of the adjective form is to describe styles that are modern or current in areas such as art, music, or literature.

The hotel was a beautiful example of contemporary architecture.

D. In a small group, discuss some of the things that make you and your contemporaries different from your parents' generation.

E. Match the inventions on the left with a contemporary invention on the right. Tell a partner how each invention changed the way people lived or worked.

.... 1. compact disc (1982)   a. telephone answering machine (1950)
.... 2. microwave oven (1947)   b. electric traffic stop light (1923)
.... 3. television (1927)   c. electric light bulb (1878)
.... 4. typewriter (1874)   d. cell phone (1982)

The verb *complement* is related to the word "complete." It is used to refer to things that go well together because, together, they make something complete or better. The adjective form is *complementary*.

*Caramel corn is good. The sweet caramel **complements** the salty popcorn.*

In this unit, complement is also used to mean "a set or group."

*It takes a **complement** of eight workers to run this restaurant.*

Note: Be careful not to confuse *complement* with *compliment*. To *compliment* someone means "to praise or express admiration for someone."

*The customer **complimented** the waiter for his excellent service.*

F. Circle the word that correctly completes each sentence. Compare answers with a partner.

1. This picture frame and that painting (*compliment / complement*) each other.

2. Maria was grateful for her teacher's (*complimentary / complementary*) remarks.

3. The tan shirt (*compliments / complements*) the brown suit.

4. Business partners should have (*complimentary / complementary*) skills so that one can manage the finances and the other can manage the employees.

STEP II VOCABULARY ACTIVITIES: Sentence Level

The phrase *in contrast* is used to show the difference between <u>two</u> people, objects, or events.

*The French fries were delicious. **In contrast**, the burger was cold and tasteless.*

Albeit (pronounced all–BE-it) is more common in written language than in speech. It is used to show a difference within <u>one</u> person, object, or event. *Albeit* is similar to "but" or "although."

*The French fries were delicious, **albeit** greasy.*

G. In your notebook, write sentences about fast-food restaurants, using each pair of items and the words in parentheses. Compare sentences with a partner.

1. wash glasses / throw away paper cups (*in contrast*)

   Restaurants wash glasses. In contrast, fast-food places throw away paper cups.

2. the burger was good / the burger was small (*albeit*)

3. broken chairs / shiny new tables (*contrast*)

4. a mother's idea of a good lunch / her little boy's idea of a good lunch (*contrasting*)

5. cola drinks 75¢ / water free (*in contrast*)

6. teen-aged girl's tiny salad / her boyfriend's enormous hamburger (*contrast*)

When you *abandon* something, you leave it because you don't want it or can't use it. Sometimes you give it up just temporarily.

*The house finally collapsed after the owners **abandoned** it many years ago.*

*The snow was so deep that drivers had to **abandon** their cars and walk home.*

To *abandon* a plan or a task means to stop before you have completed it.

*I had to **abandon** my plans to travel last summer because I got sick.*

When you *reject* something, you refuse to accept it. This verb is commonly used to refer to ideas or plans rather than objects. It is also often used to refer to people who are not accepted for jobs. The noun form is *rejection*.

*Centuries ago, people **rejected** the idea that the earth revolved around the sun.*

*Ellen offered to drive, but we all **rejected** the offer.*

*The University **rejected** Ted's application. He got a letter of **rejection** yesterday.*

H. Complete these sentences, in your notebook, with your own ideas. Use a form of *abandon* or *reject* in each one. Compare sentences in a small group.

1. In fast-food restaurant parking lots, there are paper cups and wrappers . . .
2. Babies are sensitive to new tastes, so they may . . .
3. Some fast-food restaurants tried selling vegetable burgers, but . . .
4. When the economy is slow, restaurant chains that planned to expand may . . .
5. We planned to go out to dinner, but when it started to rain . . .
6. The manager offered us a free dessert, but we . . .

READING 2

BEFORE YOU READ

Read these questions. Discuss your answers in a small group.

1. Do you know someone who owns a small business? If so, what kind of business is it?
2. What would be some good things about owning your own business? What would be some of the negative things?
3. How many retail business chains can you name? Take turns naming them.

This excerpt from a business textbook defines what a franchise is and discusses the advantages and disadvantages of owning one.

Franchising

At one time, all small retail businesses, such as clothing stores, restaurants, shoe stores, and grocery stores, were owned by individuals. They often gave the stores their own names: Lucy's
5 Dress Shop, Fred's Coffee Shop, Johnson Family Grocery. For some people, owning a business fulfilled a lifelong dream of independent ownership. For others, it continued a family business that dated back several generations.
10 These businesses used to line the streets of cities and small towns everywhere. Today, by contrast, the small independent shops are almost all gone, and chain stores like The Gap, Starbuck's, and 7-Eleven have moved
15 in to replace them. Most small independent businesses couldn't compete with the giant chains and eventually failed. However, many owners didn't abandon retail sales altogether. They became small business owners once
20 again through franchises. The franchise system is a contemporary business model that has increasingly dominated the small business sector of retail trade over the last few decades.

A typical commercial street in the past

A franchise is a legal and commercial
25 agreement between an individual and a parent company. It gives the person permission to own one of the company's franchise outlets, to use the company name, and to sell the products or services of the company. A person must apply
30 for a franchise; however, not all applicants are approved. Some may be rejected because of poor financial histories, for example. If approved, the new business owner (the franchisee) must pay a large start-up fee to the company (the franchiser)
35 and agree to follow its regulations. These regulations require complete uniformity in all of its franchises. This means that the franchiser establishes the rules for the appearance of the store, both inside and outside. It means the
40 franchisee can sell only the products or services of the parent company. It means that a "large coffee" must be the same size in every company franchise. It means that all restaurants in a franchise system must put the same number
45 of pickles on their burgers, and use identical napkins, paper cups, and food wrappers. It also means that the franchisee is graded regularly on its performance by the parent company.

Not all chain stores are franchises. Some are
50 owned and operated by the parent company. A franchise is owned by the franchisee. Restaurants are the most common franchises. On any city block you are likely to see at least one franchise restaurant, and often three or
55 four. In some shopping centers, the entire complement of stores is made up of franchises. Almost any kind of business can be franchised, including dental offices, hardware stores, hotels, gas stations, pet hospitals, tax consultants,
60 fitness centers, cleaning services, movie theaters, and child care centers.

Despite the restrictions, there are many advantages to owning a franchise. The most important advantage is the support and
65 assistance of the franchiser. For example, the franchiser can help a new owner find a good location, help plan an efficient use of floor space, and help decide on the amount of goods needed to start up the business. The franchiser also
70 provides detailed training for the owner

A typical commercial street today

and his staff in all areas of the business. Once established, the franchisee benefits from ongoing research and development by the company to keep the business up-to-date and competitive.
75 Company consultants and a network of fellow franchisees offer opportunities to discuss business problems. All these support services provide small business owners with the tools of big business, albeit not for free.
80   There are other advantages to owning a franchise. It helps to own a business that bears the name of a well-known corporation with an acknowledged reputation for good service. Customers are inclined to shop at stores with
85 familiar names, and more shoppers mean more

sales. Also, individual franchises benefit from the output of expensive advertisements paid for by the company, which might overlap with local advertising by franchisees. When this happens,
90 there is an extra benefit. Finally, the franchisee is not an employee of the company. He is a business owner, motivated to work hard to make his business successful.

The major disadvantage of the franchise model
95 is the close economic relationship among the many franchisees and the parent company. For instance, if one franchisee in the system is found guilty of cheating customers, it reflects poorly on the other franchisees in the system. As a result,
100 all the stores may lose customers. Similarly, if the company makes poor business decisions, the entire chain of franchises may be affected. Finally, the business owner must share his profits with the parent company to pay for the many support
105 services that the company provides.

The success of the franchise system has led to a great expansion in the number of small businesses all over the world. Tried first in the U.S., the franchise model has spread rapidly to other
110 countries. It has revolutionized retail business in many places, improved the economic status of individuals, and strengthened local economies.

READING COMPREHENSION

Mark each sentence as *T*(True) or *F*(False) according to the information in Reading 2. Use your dictionary to check the meaning of new words.

.... **1.** Franchising is a contemporary business model that has dominated the small business sector for a few decades.

.... **2.** A franchisee's business is rarely graded by the parent company.

.... **3.** In some shopping centers, the entire complement of stores is made up of fast-food restaurants.

.... **4.** Companies provide services to their franchise owners, albeit not for free.

.... **5.** There is a business advantage to owning a franchise that bears the name of a company with an acknowledged reputation for good service.

.... **6.** Customers are inclined to shop at stores with familiar names.

.... **7.** The number of small businesses has expanded all over the world because of the success of the franchise model.

READING STRATEGY

Preview this table. Then, in your notebook, write the answers to the questions below. Compare answers with a partner.

2005 Start-Up Costs for Selected Franchises	
Franchise	Start-Up Cost [1]
Burger King	294,000–2,800,000
Days Inn (hotels)	386,000–5,700,000
Dunkin' Donuts	179,000–1,600,000
KFC	1,100,000–1,700,000
Kumon Math & Reading Centers	10,000–30,000[2]
McDonald's	506,000–1,600,000
Midas (auto repair/maintenance)	317,000–424,000

[1] in U.S. dollars
[2] includes franchise fees

1. The start-up cost for each franchise is given as a range from the minimum cost to the maximum cost. Using the minimum costs, rank the franchises from the lowest to the highest start-up cost.

2. Using the maximum costs, rank the franchises from the lowest to the highest start-up cost.

3. Which franchise has the smallest range between its minimum and its maximum start-up costs? Which has the largest range?

4. The table does not give this information, but can you guess why Kumon's start-up costs might be so low?

5. Look at the start-up costs for Burger King. They range from two hundred ninety-four thousand dollars to two million, eight hundred thousand dollars. With a partner, take turns reading aloud the other start-up costs.

6. Amounts in the millions, such as $ 2,800,000 might be listed on a chart as $2.8 million. We say this number as: "two point eight million dollars." With a partner, read aloud all of the start-up costs over one million dollars.

STEP I VOCABULARY ACTIVITIES: Word Level

A. To *grade* something is to rate it or rank it by quality. Match the things in the left column with the grading system on the right. Then, tell a partner how the two ideas are connected.

.... 1. carpets   a. G, PG, PG-13, R

.... 2. gasoline   b. Extra Large, Large, Medium, Small

.... 3. eggs   c. A, B, C, D, F

.... 4. films   d. 87 octane, 89 octane, 93 octane

.... 5. students   e. Residential, Industrial

B. Use the target vocabulary in the box to complete this story. The words in parentheses can help you.

complement	generation	in contrast
contemporary	grade	output
expanded	had an inclination	

In 1916, a revolutionary new concept in retail sales was introduced. The first self-service grocery store, named Piggly Wiggly, opened. Shoppers of this .... were used to bringing a shopping list to a neighborhood store
(1. *shared time in history*)
and waiting while a clerk collected their groceries and measured out products like flour and rice from big barrels. .... , Piggly Wiggly customers
(2. *but*)
were given baskets and invited to serve themselves. They filled their baskets with packaged flour and rice, canned goods, and other grocery items from the shelves. Store sales increased enormously because customers .... to buy
(3. *were likely*)
more when they made their own selections. Soon Piggly Wiggly ....
(4. *increased in size*)
into a chain of stores, and other markets copied the self-service model. The .... supermarket was born, influencing not only the way people
(5. *modern*)
shopped, but also other aspects of the food business. For example, food suppliers increased their profit because their .... increased. In order to attract
(6. *production*)
customers, they used more attractive packaging to .... the better
(7. *go together with*)
.... of food they began to use. They also lowered their prices, and
(8. *quality*)
began advertising their brand named products.

To *acknowledge* something means to admit or agree that it is real or true. The noun form is *acknowledgement*.

*Sam **acknowledges** that the supermarket has lower prices, but he still prefers the small market near his house.*

C. Match the beginnings of the sentences on the left with the endings on the right to make complete sentences. Compare sentences with a partner.

.... 1. I acknowledge that English is difficult,   **a.** but I don't want one.

.... 2. I acknowledge that air travel is fast,   **b.** but I hate to cook.

.... 3. I acknowledge that exercise is good for you,   **c.** but I'm very lazy.

.... 4. I acknowledge that cats are good pets,   **d.** but I hate to fly.

.... 5. I acknowledge that it's cheaper to eat at home,   **e.** but I'm a fast learner.

When two things *overlap*, part of one thing covers part of the other. The verb *overlap* can refer to time, topic, or the position of objects in space. When two events *overlap*, the second one starts before the first one ends. When two topics *overlap with* each other, they cover part of the same subject matter. The noun form is also *overlap*.

*These two meetings **overlap**, so we need to reschedule one of them.*

*There was a lot of **overlap** between the lecture on computers and the one on Internet technology.*

*A fish's scales **overlap** each other to protect the skin beneath.*

D. Look at this schedule of history classes on Monday at State College. Then, with a partner, discuss which classes overlap in time and which overlap in subject matter. What changes do you suggest?

Class	Time
Roman History	8:00–9:30
Europe from 1850 to Present Day	9:00–10:30
The History of the Middle East	10:30–12:00
Roman and Greek History	1:30–3:00
Europe from 1800 to 1900	3:00–4:00
The History of China	3:30–5:00

STEP II VOCABULARY ACTIVITIES: Sentence Level

To *expand* means "to grow or increase." The noun form is *expansion*. The adjective form is *expansive*. It means "to cover a wide area."

*The **expansion** took nearly a year to complete.*

*People are happy with the **expansive** new parking lot at the store.*

E. Restate these sentences in your notebook, using the form of *expand* in parentheses.

1. The McDonald's menu now includes salads. (*has expanded*)

2. By 2002, the network of McDonald's franchises covered 120 foreign countries. (*expansive*)

3. Recently, McDonald's growth has been faster overseas than in the U.S. (*has been expanding*)

4. Many McDonald's franchises have added a children's play yard to increase their appeal to families. (*expand*)

Word Form Chart

Noun	Verb	Adjective	Adverb
economy economics economist	economize	economic economical economy	economically

The noun *economy* refers to the operation of a country's money supply, industry, and trade. The term *the economy* is often used to refer to the financial situation of a particular nation. The adjective form related to this meaning is *economic*.

> In a healthy **economy,** almost everyone who is able to work has a job.

> **The economy** may be weakened by recent labor strikes.

> Franchising has benefited the **economies** of many underdeveloped countries.

> **Economic** growth has slowed in recent months.

Another common use of *economy* (noun) is to refer to the careful use of time, money, and materials. The verb form related to this meaning is *economize*. The adjective form is *economical*.

> Fast-food kitchens are examples of **economy**: no food is wasted, no time is wasted.

> A restaurant might try to **economize** by serving smaller portions.

> It may not be **economical** for a store to stay open extra hours per day.

Economy is also an adjective form that is used to describe products.

> Buy the giant **economy** size. You'll save money.

Economics is the science that studies systems of production, distribution, and use of goods and services. An *economist* is an expert in economics.

> Professor Brown teaches **economics**. He is an **economist** as well as a business owner.

F. Complete the paragraph, using forms of *economy*. Compare work with a partner.

Giant retail stores make a small profit on each item they sell, but they depend on making a large number of sales. Their goods are (1) .... priced to attract customers. Shoppers are pleased that they can (2) .... by buying products in large, (3) .... sizes. They believe that it is (4) .... to buy more and pay a lower price. (5) .... have studied the effect of a giant store on the local (6) .... of cities where they are located. They believe that the (7) .... impact is great. Many small stores are forced to close because they cannot compete with the giant retailers.

> If someone *is inclined to* do/be something, it means they are likely to do/be it, based on their nature, personality, or experience. The noun form, *inclination*, can also be used to express the same meaning as the phrase *to have an inclination* (to do something).
>
> *Steve **is inclined to** be very careful with his money.*
>
> *He **has an inclination** to look for bargains whenever he goes shopping.*
>
> *She'll probably learn the piano easily because she's very musically **inclined**.*
>
> Note: *Incline* (noun, pronounced IN-cline) refers to a slope.
>
> *When parking on an **incline**, be sure to turn the wheels away from the curb.*

G. In your notebook, write sentences that include these ideas. Use a form of *incline* in each.

1. people who are very hungry / eat too much

   People who are very hungry are inclined to eat too much.

2. a teenager's eating habits / toward fast food

3. people who can't swim / (not) own sailboats

4. dogs / bark at strangers

5. little sisters / copy their big sisters

H. Self-Assessment Review: Go back to page 85 and reassess your knowledge of the target vocabulary. How has your understanding of the words changed? What words do you feel most comfortable with now?

WRITING AND DISCUSSION TOPICS

1. What are some changes that a U.S. fast-food restaurant might have to make when it opens a franchise in another country? Consider, for example, the food, the people, and the local customs.

2. What are some ways that a fast-food restaurant—or other type of business—could economize if it starts to lose money?

3. Why are small, independent retail businesses inclined to disappear when franchise stores open nearby?

4. Think about all of the fast-food restaurants you have visited. In what ways are they the same? What are some differences?

5. Many companies are now creating franchises in underdeveloped countries. Do you think these franchises help or hurt the economies of these countries? Explain your opinion.

THE AUTISM PUZZLE

In this unit, you will

- ⊃ read about a puzzling brain disorder.
- ⊃ learn how to make inferences in your reading.
- ⊃ increase your understanding of the target academic words for this unit:

appropriate	constrain	link	participate	ratio
assess	infer	mature	phase	relax
capable	interact	odd	predominant	task

SELF-ASSESSMENT OF TARGET WORDS

Think carefully about how well you know each target word in this unit. Then, write it in the appropriate column in the chart.

I have never seen the word before.	I have seen the word but am not sure what it means.	I understand the word when I see or hear it in a sentence.	I have tried to use this word, but I am not sure I am using it correctly.	I use the word with confidence in either speaking *or* writing.	I use the word with confidence, both in speaking *and* writing.

MORE WORDS YOU'LL NEED

disability: something that makes you unable to use a part of your body properly

BEFORE YOU READ

Read these questions. Discuss your answers in a small group.

1. Have you ever known anyone who has a disability? What things were they not able to do?

2. In what ways are people with disabilities just like everyone else?

3. What do you know about autism?

READ

This article blends information about autism with the story of one autistic child, Shawn. Notice how the two stories are distinguished from each other.

The Autism Puzzle

Autism is a little-understood brain disorder marked by poor social and communication skills and repetitive behavior. Meet two-year-old Shawn, who was just diagnosed with autism.

5 *Shawn sits spinning the wheels of a toy car— spinning, spinning, spinning.*

Shawn's parents now realize that spinning is not a typical **phase** of childhood, but a common repetitive behavior of autistic children.

10 *"Let's pretend we're dogs," Shawn's three-year- old cousin suggests. "Woof," she barks, walking on hands and knees. Shawn, also three, flaps his hands in front of his face.*

Autistic kids can't pretend because they're not 15 **capable** of imagining something that is not real. The **odd** hand-flapping behavior is common in kids with autism.

*"Let's go to the market," Shawn's mom says. Shawn, now four, hurries to the door and stands 20 waiting. The market is noisy with recorded music and the clatter of shopping carts. Shawn covers his ears and is soon screaming. His mom **infers** that the noise hurts his ears.*

Extreme sensitivity to loud or harsh sounds 25 is common in autism, as is sensitivity to bright lights and various textures.

Six-year-old Shawn is watching a Sesame Street videotape. "A B C," it sings. Shawn rewinds the 30 tape and it repeats, "A B C." His mother calls, "Shawn! Don't rewind the tape." He knows this isn't allowed, but he likes to see the same part over and over. "No rewind," he answers.

Like most autistic children, Shawn likes repetition, and he can't **constrain** his behavior. 35 His language skills are poorly developed, and he doesn't speak in full sentences.

Shawn's textbook asks this question: Which of these smells good? (a) a window (b) a flower (c) a lamp. Shawn lifts the book to his nose and 40 sniffs. None of them smells at all, so he leaves the answer blank.

Schools usually fail to accurately **assess** the abilities of autistic children because classroom **tasks** are not **appropriate** for them. For 45 instance, many autistic children are not able to **link** a printed word with something that is not real.

Shawn's family goes to visit Grandma and Grandpa. Shawn, now eight, rings the doorbell, 50 opens the door, and walks in. "Hi, Shawn," says Grandma. He ignores her and turns on the TV. "Did you get wet in the rain?" Grandpa asks. "Yes. Rain," Shawn answers.

Like most autistic children, Shawn doesn't 55 understand how to behave appropriately in social situations. He doesn't **interact** much with others, and prefers to be alone. He answers questions that people ask, but doesn't grasp the give-and-take of conversation.

Eleven-year-old Shawn is playing baseball. When it's his turn at bat, he hits the ball into the outfield. "Run!" yells the team coach. Shawn walks toward first base. Meanwhile, Brad picks up the ball and brings it to Shawn. Like all players on this special team, Shawn and Brad have autism.

Most participants on this team are boys. That's because kids with autism are **predominantly** male, with boys outnumbering girls by a **ratio** of 4 to 1. Autistic kids may have excellent physical skills, but they rarely **participate** in team sports because they don't understand the rules.

Shawn is doing math homework. He writes fast, and in less than five minutes he has solved 25 multiplication problems.

Shawn is very bright, but not academically **mature**. His oral language skills are poor, but in school he excels at math and spelling. He enjoys looking at photographs, and is fascinated by maps and calendars. He frequently writes letters to Grandma and Grandpa describing places his family has visited.

It's bedtime. Shawn showers and puts on pajamas. He brushes his teeth and climbs into bed. "I love you," says Mom, giving him a kiss. "I love you," says Shawn and closes his eyes.

Shawn is asleep. Finally, his handsome face and sturdy body **relax**.

READING COMPREHENSION

Mark each sentence as *T* (True) or *F* (False) according to the information in Reading 1. Use your dictionary to check the meaning of new words.

.... **1.** Shawn's parents thought that spinning was a typical phase of childhood.

.... **2.** Autistic kids are not capable of imagining something that is not real.

.... **3.** It is difficult for autistic kids to constrain their odd behavior.

.... **4.** Shawn's mother inferred that he liked the loud music in the market.

.... **5.** Autism seems to be linked to the sex of a child.

.... **6.** Autistic girls outnumber autistic boys by a ratio of 4 to 1.

.... **7.** Autistic kids seldom participate in team sports because they don't interact with other kids.

.... **8.** Schools are usually unable to assess the abilities of autistic children because classroom tasks are not appropriate for them.

.... **9.** Autistic kids may be bright, but they are not academically mature.

.... **10.** Autistic kids are predominantly male, so most of them have excellent physical skills.

.... **11.** Autistic children can relax when they are sleeping.

READING STRATEGY: Making Inferences

To *infer* is to use indirect information or evidence to come to a decision or a logical conclusion. Parents of an autistic child must often use *inference* to understand their child's behavior because the child may not be able to explain what he wants or what he doesn't like. For example, in Reading 1, there is a sentence:

*In the market, Shawn covers his ears and is soon screaming. His mom **infers** that the noise hurts his ears.*

Shawn's mother *made an inference* based on what she saw. Maybe she was correct, or maybe she wasn't, but it was a logical conclusion.

Read these excerpts from Reading 1. What can you infer from the information? More than one answer may be possible.

1. "Let's go to the market," Shawn's mom says. Shawn walks to the door and stands waiting.
   ...✓... **a.** Shawn understands his mother's words.
   ...✓... **b.** Shawn obeys his mother.
   .... **c.** Shawn is in a good mood today.

2. Shawn rewinds the tape and it plays again.
   .... **a.** Shawn knows how to operate a tape player.
   .... **b.** Shawn likes to sing along with the tape.
   .... **c.** Shawn likes the ABC song.

3. "Which of these smells good?" Shawn lifts the book to his nose and sniffs. None of them smells at all.
   .... **a.** Shawn has a poor sense of smell.
   .... **b.** Shawn can read.
   .... **c.** Shawn expected the words to smell.

4. "Did you get wet in the rain?" Grandpa asks. "Yes. Rain," Shawn answers.
   .... **a.** Shawn likes the rain.
   .... **b.** Shawn likes Grandpa.
   .... **c.** Shawn understands Grandpa's question.

5. "Let's pretend we're dogs," Shawn's three-year-old cousin suggests.
   .... **a.** Shawn's three-year-old cousin can talk.
   .... **b.** Shawn's three-year-old cousin can pretend.
   .... **c.** Shawn's three-year-old cousin has a dog.

STEP I VOCABULARY ACTIVITIES: Word Level

A. Read this article that gives advice to parents of autistic children. Use the target vocabulary in the box to complete the article. Compare results with a partner.

appropriate	capabilities	interact	participate	relax
assess	constrain	mature	phases	task

Experts recommend that parents enroll young children with autism in a special preschool class as early as possible. The goal is to help the children strengthen their social and language skills during the formative .... of childhood
(1. *time periods*)
and learn .... classroom behavior before they enter kindergarten.
(2. *proper*)
Each day, the children .... in games, songs, and play activities
(3. *take part*)
that encourage them to .... with each other. Individual children
(4. *mix together*)
are assigned a daily ...., such as feeding the class turtle, to help
(5. *small job*)
teach responsibility. Parents are required to attend classes with their child to learn more about autistic behavior. Observing their own child in a group setting allows them to realistically .... the child's ....
(6. *judge*)   (7. *strengths*)
and limitations. Parents also see techniques that the trained teachers use to

.... a child's unwanted behavior, such as hand-flapping. Telling a
(8. *limit*)
child to .... by taking a deep breath is one technique parents learn.
(9. *become less tense*)
As the children ...., they will remember this relaxation technique
(10. *grow up*)
and use it to constrain their own behavior without being reminded.

B. A *link* is a connection between two things. Working with a partner, put a check (✓) next to the behaviors that are linked to autism, according to Reading 1.

.... **a.** spinning .... **d.** being sensitive to loud noises .... **g.** excelling at math

.... **b.** writing letters .... **e.** watching a videotape .... **h.** hand-flapping

.... **c.** pretending .... **f.** preferring to be alone .... **i.** liking repetition

C. A *phase* is a step or stage of development. Look at the phases of language development in children. Number them in the order they are likely to occur, with the first phase as *1*.

.... **a.** one-word sentences ("Ball.") .... **d.** two-word sentences ("Mama look.")

.... **b.** babbling ("Dadadada") .... **e.** three-word sentences ("Daddy, read me.")

.... **c.** cooing ("Oooooooo") .... **f.** crying

The adjective *odd* refers to something that is unusual or inappropriate for a particular situation.

*Hand-flapping is an **odd** behavior of autistic kids.*

Another meaning for *odd* applies to numbers. An odd number cannot be divided evenly by 2, such as the numbers 1, 3, 5, 7, 9, 11, 13, etc.

*I always seem to have an **odd** number of socks in my drawer.*

As a plural noun, *odds* refer to the chances of something happening.

*The **odds** are one in a million that you will win the lottery.*

*I wouldn't give you good **odds** on finding a taxi at this hour of night.*

D. Which of these would you consider an odd drink? Put a check (✓) next to them. Discuss your choices with a partner.

.... coffee with sugar .... coffee with mustard .... milk with honey

.... tea with honey .... coffee with milk .... milk with cola

.... tea with garlic .... tea with lemon .... hot chocolate with chili pepper

STEP II VOCABULARY ACTIVITIES: Sentence Level

Word Form Chart			
Noun	Verb	Adjective	Adverb
assessment reassessment	assess reassess	assessable	....

E. To *assess* something is to judge it or to form an opinion about it. Complete this paragraph about autism assessment by using a form of *assess* in each blank.

By age two, a typical child has developed many verbal and social skills, such as speaking and interacting with others. If these skills are absent, the child's doctor may suspect autism. There is not just a single test a doctor can use to (1) .... a child for autism. Instead, the doctor looks for the presence or absence of certain behaviors. Autism is (2) .... only by carefully observing the behavior of a child, so the actual (3) .... may take several hours. The doctor (4) .... the child's attempts to communicate with his parents. He also looks for repetitive behavior, such as hand-flapping, or sensitivity to sounds or textures. If the doctor's diagnosis is autism, he may suggest a (5) .... by a second doctor to confirm the diagnosis. Over the next several years the child will be (6) .... regularly to see if he has made progress.

F. A *task* is a small job, often one that is assigned by a teacher, parent, or boss. Using what you know of Shawn's skills from Reading 1, infer which of these classroom tasks will probably be difficult for him and which he will do easily. Write sentences in your notebook about each task.

1. writing about his vacation

   Shawn can probably do this task. He often writes letters to his grandparents about places he visited with his family.

2. taking a spelling test

3. solving subtraction problems

4. working with a committee to plan a class party

5. giving an oral report

The adjective *appropriate* refers to something that is suitable, proper, or correct for a particular situation. People sometimes disagree about what is appropriate or inappropriate. The noun form is *appropriateness*.

   *What is **appropriate** to wear to a job interview?*

   *Meg is **appropriately** dressed in a suit. Jeans and a t-shirt are **inappropriate**.*

   *The interviewer commented on the **inappropriateness** of Sam's clothes.*

As a verb, appropriate means "to decide to give something, especially money, for a particular purpose." The noun form is *appropriation*. This meaning is rather formal and official.

   *The university **appropriated** one million dollars for a new autism study.*

   *The business plan includes an **appropriation** for local charities.*

G. Read these short conversations. Some of Sam's responses are odd. Write a sentence about the appropriateness of Sam's reply using the word in parentheses.

1. Mark: "Thank you for the birthday card."

   Sam: "How old are you?"

   (*appropriate*) *A more appropriate response is "You're welcome."*

2. Mark: "Are you coming to my party tonight?"

   Sam: "Thank you."

   (*appropriately*) ....

3. Mark: "Can I borrow your pen?"

   Sam: "Please."

   (*inappropriate*) ....

4. Mark: "Have you seen my brother?"

   Sam: "No, I haven't."

   (*appropriate*) ....

BEFORE YOU READ

Read these questions. Discuss your answers in a small group.

1. Think of some common illnesses. What causes them?

2. Think of some common illnesses. How are they cured?

3. Why might a pharmaceutical company be willing to fund research into the causes of autism?

READ

This article details some of the current research into autism and some possible causes for it.

Looking for Answers

Autism is a neurological disorder that usually appears before a child's third birthday. It is marked by impaired language skills, impaired social skills, and repetitive behaviors.

5 Recently there has been a dramatic and unexplained increase in the number of children diagnosed with autism. Medical scientists estimate an autism ratio of 1 in every 150 children in the United States; others estimate 1 in 500.
10 Both figures are alarming, especially considering that scientists do not know what causes autism and do not know how to cure it. Medical researchers have been looking for answers.

Scientists use the term "autism spectrum" to
15 refer to the range of capabilities that autistic people display. At one extreme of the spectrum, individuals are severely affected, while at the other extreme, individuals are only mildly affected. Some individuals cannot speak; others
20 are highly verbal. Some are overly sensitive to noise; others seem not to notice it. Some prefer to be alone; others want friends. Some even marry and have children. Some are unable to learn school subjects; others go on to acquire a
25 Ph.D. degree. Indeed, each person with autism may have a unique set of traits.

Although scientists agree on the traits that characterize autism, they have not yet found

what causes autism. In the 1950s, autism was
30 considered a psychological disorder, caused by "refrigerator mothers." Their personalities were thought to be so cold and uncaring that their children grew up unable to speak or interact with others. As research progressed, scientists realized
35 that autism was actually a neurological, or brain, disorder. Studies have identified several areas of the brain that differ from the norm in autistic individuals. These areas involve emotions, critical thinking, learning, and paying attention.
40 However, no one area seems to hold the key to autism. Some researchers have inferred that faulty[1] neural connections between areas of the brain may be responsible for autism. Or perhaps there are too many connections, resulting in an
45 overload of messages within the brain.

Medical scientists have also explored brain chemistry. In a recent study, researchers took blood samples from many newborns. When some of these babies later developed autism, the
50 researchers tested their early blood samples and found high levels of four chemicals that influence the early phases of brain development. However, they have not been able to prove a direct link between the chemicals and the autism.

55 There is strong agreement that genes, carriers of inherited traits, play a role in autism, and research continues to explore heredity as a cause. Recently, researchers found a link

[1] *faulty*: not working correctly

between autism and the age of the child's father, with the odds of parenting an autistic child increasing with older fathers. It is also known that among autistic children, males predominate by a ratio of 4 to 1, and that autism seems to run in families. Despite the strong hereditary evidence, scientists have yet to identify a single gene responsible for autism. They now think that a combination of 10 or more faulty genes may trigger autism.

Scientists are also investigating environmental causes. They have looked into toxic metals in water and soil, harmful chemicals in household products, viruses, air pollution, and even television viewing, but have not found a consistent link to autism.

Despite this extensive research, scientists have been unsuccessful in finding either a cause or a cure for autism. However, treatment, either through medication or training, has benefited many autistic children by helping them to relax, to constrain antisocial behavior, to participate socially, and to learn useful skills. Medication has worked for some children, but it has not been widely used because it can have serious side effects. Other treatments that have worked for some children include controlling the child's diet, providing the child with a companion dog, and encouraging self-expression through art.

The most common training is Applied Behavior Analysis, which breaks down a task into tiny steps and rewards every small success with a bit of cookie or other treat. If a child does not speak, for example, the therapist will reward even a small sound while repeating a word that she wants the child to say. It may take several sessions to get the child to utter a sound, and many more to get him to say a word, but each success is praised and rewarded. Many autistic children have improved greatly with such training, but others have not.

Whatever treatment parents decide is appropriate, they must be aware that children are most likely to benefit if they begin early. Delaying treatment until the child matures is a waste of valuable time. Parents must also recognize that not all treatments benefit every child, so they must regularly assess their child's behavior for signs of progress. Treatment that doesn't work is also a waste of time.

Meanwhile, scientists are still looking for answers to solve the autism puzzle.

READING COMPREHENSION

Mark each statement as *T* (True) or *F* (False) according to the information in Reading 2. Use your dictionary to check the meaning of new words.

.... 1. Researchers found four chemicals that influence the early phases of brain development.

.... 2. As a man gets older, the odds increase that he will parent an autistic child.

.... 3. There is strong agreement that heredity is the predominant cause of autism.

.... 4. Researchers have found a link between autism and television viewing.

.... 5. Medication has helped some autistic children constrain their behavior.

.... 6. Children who participate in Applied Behavior Analysis learn a task one step at a time.

.... 7. Parents must regularly assess their child's behavior for signs that they are wasting time.

READING STRATEGY

Reread the paragraphs indicated. Then, write *D* for the ideas that are directly stated and *I* for those that you can infer. Write *N* if an idea is neither directly stated nor inferable. Discuss your answers in a small group.

Paragraph 2

_D_ **1.** Scientists do not know the cause of autism.

.... **2.** There is no cure for autism.

_I_ **3.** Scientists cannot explain the recent increase in autism.

.... **4.** Scientists are not sure how many children are affected.

.... **5.** Scientists are alarmed.

Paragraph 3

.... **1.** A person who is mildly affected with autism is highly verbal.

.... **2.** Some people with autism are very intelligent.

.... **3.** Not all autistic people prefer to be alone.

.... **4.** The term "autism spectrum" was recently created.

.... **5.** Each autistic person may have a different combination of traits.

Paragraph 4

.... **1.** Autism is not a psychological disorder.

.... **2.** A neurological disorder is a disorder involving the brain.

.... **3.** Scientists are not certain if faulty neural connections cause autism.

.... **4.** Scientists have abandoned their study of the brain.

.... **5.** Several areas in the brain of autistic children differ from those in normal kids.

STEP I VOCABULARY ACTIVITIES: Word Level

> A person who is *capable* of doing something has the necessary skills to do it. If he lacks these skills, then he is *incapable* of doing it. The words can also refer to objects.
>
> *Most autistic children are **incapable** of imagining something that is not real.*
>
> *Passenger airplanes are **capable** of flying overseas without refueling.*

A. Which of these activities is a blind person capable of doing? Mark them with a *C* for capable or an *I* for incapable. Then, use the items to describe the capabilities of a blind person to a partner.

*A blind person has the **capability** to listen to music.*

_C_ listening to music .... riding on a bus .... telling jokes

.... driving a car .... reading a newspaper .... using a telephone

> To *relax* means to stop working and rest. It can also mean to make your body less tense by loosening your muscles.
>
> *When he sleeps, Shawn can finally relax and get some rest.*
>
> To *relax* <u>something</u> means to make it looser or more flexible.
>
> *Teachers often relax classroom rules for students with disabilities.*

B. Complete each sentence with *relax* or *relax it*.

1. I've worked hard all day. It's time to .... relax ....

2. Sometimes you can cure a headache if you just ....

3. The law against speeding is too strict. I wish the government would
....

4. Don't pull the rope so tight. Can you please .... ?

5. I often play the piano to ....

Word Form Chart			
Noun	Verb	Adjective	Adverb
constrain constraints	constrain	constrained unconstrained	....

C. To *constrain* someone or something is to hold them back or limit their actions. Put a check (✓) next to the behaviors that you think parents should constrain in their children. Discuss your choices with a partner.

.... **1.** studying   .... **4.** playing   .... **7.** laughing

.... **2.** screaming   .... **5.** watching TV   .... **8.** arguing

.... **3.** sleeping   .... **6.** fighting   .... **9.** surfing the Web

D. The plural noun *constraints* is a more formal way of describing limits. Match the formal language with its more informal version.

.... **1.** I have financial constraints.   **a.** My husband doesn't want me to.

.... **2.** I have medical constraints.   **b.** I have to finish this by tomorrow.

.... **3.** I have time constraints.   **c.** My car won't start.

.... **4.** I have transportation constraints. **d.** I can't afford that right now.

.... **5.** I have marital constraints.   **e.** I need to see a lawyer about this.

.... **6.** There are legal constraints to   **f.** I'm not healthy enough to do that.
selling my house.

Word Form Chart			
Noun	Verb	Adjective	Adverb
maturation maturity immaturity	mature	mature immature maturational	....

To *mature* refers to the process of becoming fully developed physically or mentally. If someone or something is *immature*, then development is delayed compared to others.

> As boys **mature**, they become taller and more muscular.

> Susan is ten, but she's so **immature**.

There are two noun forms:

maturation   the process of developing or aging
maturity   the state of being fully developed

E. Read this paragraph. Then, complete it by using the correct form of *mature* from the chart. Compare answers with a partner.

A premature baby is one that is born before it is fully developed. Because of its (1) ...., a premature baby is usually placed in a hospital incubator where it can continue to (2) .... in a safe environment. A baby born too soon has not had time for adequate (3) .... of body systems that are essential for life. The baby's (4) .... lungs, for example, may not be able to supply enough oxygen, so it will need help breathing. The baby will remain in the incubator until it has achieved a safe level of (5) .... The baby will make steady progress, but its growth will be delayed compared to that of a full-term baby. For example, a full-term baby may sit up at six months of age, but a premature infant may not reach this (6) .... phase for several more months.

Word Form Chart			
Noun	Verb	Adjective	Adverb
predominance	predominate*	predominant	predominantly

*Note: There is no *-ing* form for this verb.

F. Read the paragraph about Temple Grandin. Then, rewrite the sentences that follow in your notebook, using the form of *predominant* in parentheses.

Temple Grandin is autistic, yet she has a Ph.D. and is a university professor. Dr. Grandin has written several books about autism. Her superior verbal skills and intelligence have enabled her to analyze and describe how individuals with autism think. She writes, "I think in pictures. Words are like a second language to me. I translate both spoken and written words into full-color movies."

1. Among high-functioning autistic individuals, most are visual thinkers. (*predominance*)

    There is a predominance of visual thinkers among high-functioning autistic people.

2. Nouns are easiest because they are mostly things you can picture. (*predominantly*)

3. Most people are verbal thinkers in universities. (*predominate*)

4. Dr. Grandin was surprised by the number of people who think only in words. (*predominance*)

5. Seeing pictures in her mind is the way Temple Grandin creates ideas. (*predominant*)

G. A *ratio* is a mathematical expression comparing the size or amount of two sets of things. Write a sentence in your notebook to express the ratios of these groups. Discuss your sentences in a small group.

1. hand predominance: right-handed, 9; left-handed, 1

    Right-handed people outnumber left-handed people by a ration of 9 to 1.
    (meaning, for every 10 people, 9 are right-handed and 1 is left-handed)

2. at birth: boys, 105; girls, 100

3. autistic children: girls, 1; boys, 4

4. adults who are colorblind: men, 15; women, 1

5. at age 65: women, 10; men, 7

6. people in my family: male, ...; female, ...

7. communication I receive: email, ...; phone calls ....

8. school time: hours in class, ...; hours studying, ...

Word Form Chart			
Noun	Verb	Adjective	Adverb
participate participation	participate	participatory	....

H. Read this description of an autism study. Then, complete the paragraph by using the correct form of *participate* in each blank. Compare answers with a partner.

Several young children are asked to (1) .... in an experiment. Half of the (2) .... are typical children, and half of the (3) .... are autistic children. Their (4) .... consists of watching a scene in which two little girls are playing with dolls. One of the girls, Mary, puts her doll in a basket and leaves the room. While she is gone, her friend, Linda, takes the doll out of the basket and puts it into the drawer of a table. Then Mary returns. The children who are (5) .... in the experiment are asked, "Where will Mary look for her doll?" The typical children agree that Mary will look in the basket because that's where she left the doll. However, the autistic children say that Mary will look in the drawer because the doll is there now. This (6) .... experiment demonstrates that autistic kids cannot imagine something that is not true.

I. Self-Assessment Review: Go back to page 99 and reassess your knowledge of the target vocabulary. How has your understanding of the words changed? What words do you feel most comfortable with now?

WRITING AND DISCUSSION TOPICS

1. Why might it be difficult to be friends with an autistic person? What would be some of the challenges?

2. The first reading is called "The Autism Puzzle." Why is this a good title?

3. What are some facts you learned about autism?

4. The second reading mentions three alternative treatments for autism (controlling the child's diet, providing him with a companion dog, and encouraging self-expression through art). How might each of these treatments help children with autism?

SEA OF LIFE

In this unit, you will

⊃ learn about the health of Earth's oceans and deep-sea life.

⊃ learn how to read and interpret statistical tables.

⊃ increase your understanding of the target academic words for this unit:

aggregate	conduct	finite	process	trace
annual	contribute	impact	temporary	ultimate
compatible	erode	occupy	terminate	

SELF-ASSESSMENT OF TARGET WORDS

Think carefully about how well you know each target word in this unit. Then, write it in the appropriate column in the chart.

I have never seen the word before.	I have seen the word but am not sure what it means.	I understand the word when I see or hear it in a sentence.	I have tried to use this word, but I am not sure I am using it correctly.	I use the word with confidence in either speaking *or* writing.	I use the word with confidence, both in speaking *and* writing.

MORE WORDS YOU'LL NEED

nutrient: a substance that provides nourishment to animals or plants

deplete: reduce the amount of something, usually refers to natural resources

depletion: the act of reducing something, usually natural resources

BEFORE YOU READ

Read these questions. Discuss your answers in a small group.

1. How often do you eat fish?
2. Do you ever visit the ocean to go fishing or to relax on a beach?
3. How do oceans benefit people?

READ

This article details the current threats to the oceans and offers suggestions for curbing the destruction.

Saving the Oceans

The oceans of the world **occupy** over 70% of the earth's surface. They provide food for billions of people, serve as places of recreation, and facilitate the transportation of passengers
5   and cargo. For all of human history, people regarded the oceans as an indestructible and **infinite** resource. Until recently, humans had little **impact** on the oceans. However, as the earth's population increases, human activity will
10 **ultimately** destroy the oceans unless immediate steps are taken.

Over-fishing is one major threat. Fish are being taken out of the oceans faster than the remaining fish can reproduce. A big fish—tuna,
15 cod, shark, or swordfish—yields many pounds of delicious seafood when it reaches maturity. However, to meet the increasing demand for these fish, commercial fishermen began catching small, immature fish. In the **process**, they
20 depleted the species. Ocean scientists estimate that 90% of these big fish are now gone from the oceans, and about 30% of all fished species have been destroyed.

Of the earth's 6.5 billion people, over one
25 billion rely on fish as a source of protein. Billions more eat fish frequently because of its health benefits and its good taste. Throughout the world, food from the sea provides between 5% and 10% of the total food supply. But when
30 fish disappear from the oceans, they will also disappear from our dinner plates. The impact on those who rely on fish could be malnutrition or even starvation.

Humans are impacting ocean life not only
35 by what they take out of the oceans, but also by what they put into the oceans. Carelessly discarded cans, bottles, plastic cups, and baby diapers find their way into the stomachs of fish, often killing them. Toxic chemicals and
40 industrial trash are also discarded into the oceans, either accidentally or thoughtlessly. Such **conduct** pollutes the water and kills sea life. Spills from a single oil tanker can **contribute** 200,000 tons of oil to the already
45 polluted oceans. In the United States, an estimated 15,000 tons of automobile oil **annually** washes off roads into rivers and streams and ultimately into the sea.

Along with the harmful oil, however, run-
50 off also carries tons of nutrients in the form

2004 HIGHEST OCEAN HARVESTS
(In millions of tons)

COUNTRY	HARVEST	COUNTRY	HARVEST
Chile	5.9	Peru	10.5
China	16.3	Russia	3.1
India	3.1	South Korea	1.7
Indonesia	5.0	Thailand	2.9
Japan	4.9	United States	5.5
Norway	2.9	**World Total**	81.6

of plant matter, fertilizers, animal waste, and garbage that can be **traced** to cities, farms, factories, and forests. These nutrients may seem like a good thing at first, but poisonous algae and bacteria (microscopic plants and animals) in the ocean feed on the nutrients. As the run-off increases, the **aggregation** of algae and bacteria increases, further **eroding** the marine environment. Small fish that feed on the algae and bacteria are sickened or killed by the poisons they contain. When larger fish feed on the smaller ones, they too are sickened by the poisons. Ultimately, humans who eat the flesh of poisoned fish will be sickened, too.

Are healthy oceans **compatible** with an industrialized world? What can be done to **terminate** the steady destruction of the oceans? Among other steps, countries can set limits on the number of fish that fishermen can legally catch. Governments can also create sea reserves, areas where fishing is **temporarily** banned until the fish population increases. Commercial enterprises can develop open-ocean aquaculture to grow fish in underwater cages miles from land. And individuals can refuse to buy fish in restaurants and markets if the species is threatened.

Governments can also protect the sea by enacting strict controls on ocean dumping. They can demand that oil tankers have higher safety standards. They can process run-off water to remove toxic substances. Individuals can properly dispose of leftover household and garden chemicals so they do not add to the toxic run-off into the oceans.

Scientists agree that it's not too late to save the oceans, but we must begin at once to take the necessary steps.

READING COMPREHENSION

Mark each sentence as *T* (True) or *F* (False) according to the information in Reading 1. Use your dictionary to check the meaning of new words.

.... 1. Humans had little impact on the oceans until recently.

.... 2. Humans occupy over 70% of the earth's surface.

.... 3. For all of human history, people thought of the oceans as a resource that was infinite and indestructible.

.... 4. Steps must be taken to terminate human activity that may ultimately erode the quality of the oceans.

.... 5. Over-fishing may temporarily benefit certain species of fish.

.... 6. The conduct of discarding trash into the oceans greatly contributes to pollution.

.... 7. Increases in the aggregation of algae and bacteria can be traced to the nutrients in run-off from cities, farms, factories, and forests.

.... 8. Oil tankers annually spill 200,000 tons of oil into the oceans.

.... 9. It isn't possible to process run-off water to remove toxic substances.

.... 10. Healthy oceans are compatible with an industrialized world if necessary steps are taken to protect the oceans.

READING STRATEGY: Reading Statistical Tables

Articles about scientific topics frequently contain statistics that support the information in the text. The table in Reading 1, for example, compares the amount of fish collected, or harvested, by several nations of the world to support the information about overfishing.

Numerical information in tables is often reduced for clarity. The table in Reading 1 eliminates the many zeros in the numbers by telling the reader that amounts are in million tons. So, for Chile, the number 5.9 really means that Chile harvested 5,900,000 tons of fish. Shortened numbers are read differently from complete numbers. Chile's harvest is read "five point nine million tons."

Numbers in tables are also often rounded up or down. The actual number of fish might be 5,833,214 tons, for example, but that number is rounded up to 5.9 million tons.

A. With a partner, do these activities. Use the information in the table in Reading 1.

1. In the order of their fish harvests, read all of the country names and their fish harvests out loud. Use shortened numbers, such as "Chile—five point nine million tons."

2. From biggest harvest to smallest, write all of the complete numbers, such as 5,900,000. Then, read them out loud.

B. What can you infer from the information in the table? Mark a statement _I_ if you can infer that it is true. Mark a statement _N_ if you cannot infer that it is true.

_N_ **a.** The United States harvested more fish in 2004 than in 2003.

.... **b.** Fishing is an important industry in these countries.

.... **c.** About half of the top countries are in Asia.

.... **d.** India harvested more fish than Norway.

.... **e.** The numbers do not include fish caught in rivers and lakes.

.... **f.** All the fish is eaten by people within the country that harvests it.

.... **g.** China harvested about 20% of the world total in 2004.

.... **h.** Canada did not harvest fish in 2004.

STEP I VOCABULARY ACTIVITIES: Word Level

A. Use the target vocabulary in this unit to complete these analogies. Then write the type of relationship each analogy has: example, synonym, antonym, action, or part. (See Unit 1, page 11, for more on analogies.)

	Relationship
1. start : end AS begin :	....
2. house : permanent AS tent :	....
3. grow : build AS destroy :	....
4. player : team AS part :	....
5. phase : development AS step :	....

B. *Erosion* **is the gradual process of something being destroyed or wearing away. It can describe natural or biological processes or more abstract ideas. With a partner, decide what might be responsible for eroding these things.**

1. mountains

2. the soil next to a river

3. a person's hopes about something

4. the pavement on a street

5. a person's enjoyment of movies

6. a person's respect for a leader

> The verb *aggregate* (pronounced AG-gre-GATE, with a slight stress on the last syllable) means to collect items into one body or mass.
>
> *The company will* **aggregate** *its small stores into one super store.*
>
> The adjective form is spelled the same way but is pronounced slightly differently (AG-gre-gate, no stress on the last syllable).
>
> *The* **aggregate** *effect of pollution is depletion of sea life.*
>
> The noun has two forms: *aggregate* (pronounced like the adjective) and *aggregation*.

C. With a partner, decide what to call an aggregation of these items. More than one answer is possible.

1. an aggregation of stores: _a shopping mall, a shopping center, a strip mall_

2. an aggregation of books: ....

3. an aggregation of plants: ....

4. an aggregation of people: ....

5. an aggregation of printed pages: ....

D. An annual event is one that occurs once a year or is repeated every year. Which of these occur annually? Put a check (✓) next to them. When in the year do they take place?

.... spring .... your birthday .... new classes

.... New Year's Day .... a wedding .... animal migration

.... a full moon .... October .... family gatherings

When something is *finite* (pronounced FI-nite, rhyming with SKY-light), it is fixed in space or amount and can be measured.

*The amount of oil in the world is **finite**. When we use it up, there is no more.*

Something *infinite* (pronounced IN-fi-nit) is without limits. This word is often used for something that seems endless, very great, or not measurable.

*She is **infinitely** patient with the children in her class.*

E. Match each sentence in the left column with one in the right column that has the same meaning.

.... **1.** I have a finite amount of money to spend. **a.** I only have a few days off.

.... **2.** I am infinitely more qualified than you. **b.** I can't pay any more than this.

.... **3.** I have an infinite number of friends. **c.** I really admire them.

.... **4.** I have infinite respect for teachers. **d.** I can do it better.

.... **5.** I have a finite number of vacation days. **e.** I know a lot of people.

F. Use the target vocabulary in the box to complete this article on the impact of global warming. Compare results with a partner.

annual	erosion	traced
compatible	impact	ultimately
contributed	process	

Today there are 20,000 to 25,000 polar bears worldwide. This represents a decline of 21% since 1997 that can be directly (1) .... to global warming. As the average (2) .... ocean temperature in the Arctic rises, the bear population declines. The bears' way of life is not (3) .... with a warm climate because they depend on sea ice for summer hunting. The (4) .... of global warming has caused an (5) .... of the polar bear environment. It has (6) .... to weight loss in the males, falling reproduction rates in the females, and lower survival rates among newborn cubs. If the (7) .... of global warming continues at its present rate, the polar bears will (8) .... disappear.

STEP II VOCABULARY ACTIVITIES: Sentence Level

> When people or things are *compatible*, they get along well or work together well. The negative form is *incompatible*. The noun forms are *compatibility* and *incompatibility*.
>
> *Tom and Linda got a divorce because they feel they are not **compatible**.*
>
> *Electrical appliances are often **incompatible** with foreign power systems.*

G. Imagine that you have an old Apple computer. You need some new equipment and software. In your notebook, write four questions you might ask a store clerk, using *compatible*, *compatibility*, *incompatible*, and *incompatibility* one time each.

> *Are there compatibility problems with these new printers and older computers?*

> The word *impact* has two meanings. It can refer to a strong force hitting something or, more abstractly, to the effect something has or creates. Both meanings have a noun and verb form.
>
> *We felt the **impact** of the explosion a mile away.*
>
> *The conduct of oil companies **impacts** all our lives.*

H. In your notebook, rewrite each sentence two ways using *impact* as a noun and a verb. Compare sentences with a partner.

1. High winds had an effect on air traffic yesterday.

   High winds impacted air traffic yesterday.

   High winds had an impact on air traffic yesterday.

2. Her new job affected the whole family.

3. The collision had a different effect on each of us.

4. The new law will change the way people pay their taxes.

I. Imagine you have just moved into your own apartment for the first time. Your friends and family have contributed different things to help set you up. Write sentences describing what they gave using the word in parentheses.

1. Your aunt / a used coffee maker (contributed)

2. Your dad / a small bookcase (contribution)

3. Your brother / three red pillows (contributor)

4. Your mom / a frying pan (contributed)

5. Your best friend / three posters (is contributing)

BEFORE YOU READ

Read these questions. Discuss your answers in a small group.

1. Some people claim that we know more about the moon than we know about our oceans. Do you agree?

2. What is the value of exploring the ocean floors?

3. Who should pay for exploring the oceans? Why?

Metric conversions for measurements used in Reading 2:

1 inch = 2.54 centimeters   1 pound = 0.45 kilograms

1 foot = 0.3 meters   1 knot = 1.85 km/hour

1 mile = 1.6 kilometers

READ

This article is about the amazing things that Alvin has seen and learned, and what Alvin can teach us.

Exploring the Deep Ocean

Alvin can dive to ocean depths of 14,764 feet—nearly three miles down. Alvin can rest on the ocean bottom or hover at middle depths for up to ten hours, taking photographs and
5 performing underwater experiments. Alvin is amazing. Many of the 150 to 200 dives Alvin makes annually result in underwater discoveries of unusual sights never before seen.

Alvin is not a man. Alvin is a deep-sea
10 submersible craft capable of carrying up to three occupants. It is owned and operated by the Woods Hole Oceanographic Institution on the east coast of the United States. Alvin was built in 1964, but it has been upgraded
15 and reconstructed many times since then. Alvin's titanium hull, or outside shell, is built to withstand the immense pressure of the deep ocean. Alvin weighs 37,400 pounds and is 23 feet 4 inches long. It has a 6-mile range and a
20 top cruising speed of 2 knots. Five hydraulic thrusters propel the craft, and lead-acid batteries power the electrical system.

Inside is an infinite variety of the latest electronic equipment, including a gyrocompass,
25 a magnometer, and a computer.

Alvin explores the ocean depths.

Alvin allows researchers to conduct underwater biological, chemical, and geological studies. Special lamps shine light into the black water so observers can see the wonders of the underwater
30 environment. Cameras are mounted on the outside to take underwater photographs, and two external "arms" enable researchers to collect underwater samples.

One day in 1977, Alvin contributed to an
35 amazing discovery. On that day, Alvin was

transporting scientists on a routine study. The craft was one and a half miles below the surface of the sea near the coast of the Galapagos Islands. As they looked through the three 12-inch portholes, the scientists were temporarily stunned to see a strange underwater landscape littered with what looked like chimneys. The chimneys were discharging clouds of black smoke into the surrounding water. Clustered around the chimneys were odd creatures that lived totally cut off from the world of sunlight. The scientists were looking at hydrothermal vents and the strange sea creatures that exist near them—an entire system of life based not on sunlight, but on energy from the earth itself.

An unusual kind of animal life lives around these vents. Among the chemicals pouring out of the vents is hydrogen sulfide, a gas that is poisonous to most land-based life. However, bacteria in the seawater near the vents feed on this gas and other dissolved chemicals and minerals pouring from the vents. Then tiny animals feed on the bacteria, and these tiny animals in turn become food for still larger animals. Giant red and white tube worms eight feet tall cluster near the vents and dominate the scene. Tiny shrimps and white crabs feed on the worms while giant clams rest in the sand. In an environment that seems incompatible with life, these creatures are thriving.

Since the first vent was discovered in 1977, hundreds of other vents have been located in oceans around the world. Some of the sites are inaccessible, so scientists have not been able to study them all. However, scientists are planning to trace the development of vents by revisiting some they studied earlier. They want to find out how long vents remain active and if the odd creatures change over time.

READING COMPREHENSION

Mark each statement as *T* (True) or *F* (False) according to the information in Reading 2. Use your dictionary to check the meaning of new words.

.... **1.** Alvin makes between 150–200 dives annually.

.... **2.** Alvin is a man who temporarily helped researchers conduct underwater studies aboard a submersible craft.

.... **3.** Alvin's occupants have an infinite variety of electronic equipment available.

.... **4.** Alvin contributed to the discovery of the Galapagos Islands in 1977.

.... **5.** Near vents, giant tube worms, shrimps, and crabs exist in an environment that seems incompatible with life.

.... **6.** Scientists plan to revisit some of the vents in order to trace their development.

.... **7.** Scientists will terminate their study of vents because some vents are inaccessible.

READING STRATEGY

Facts about numbers are often difficult to read when they are included as part of the text of an article. For this reason, scientists and technicians usually create a specification sheet, or "spec sheet," to isolate these numbers.

Using information from Reading 2, complete this spec sheet about Alvin. You may use the system of measurement in the article or convert those numbers to the metric system.

Alvin General Specifications	
Length	
Weight	
Maximum Depth	
Maximum Speed	
Range	
Occupants	
Propulsion	
Electrical System	
Equipment (Internal)	
Equipment (External)	

STEP I VOCABULARY ACTIVITIES: Word Level

Something *temporary* exists or is used for only a short time. *Temporarily* is the adverb form.

> My **temporary** driver's license is valid for only two weeks.

> The oven is **temporarily** out of order. They're going to fix it next week.

A temporary job, or *temp job*, refers to work that a person may do for a short time. This person, a *temp* or *temp worker*, is not a regular employee of the company. Usually he or she works for a *temp agency* that finds the short-term jobs for them. Some people prefer *to temp*, or work temp jobs, because they need the flexibility.

> I'm starting school in the fall, so I think I'm going to **temp** until then.

A. Which of these are temporary? Put a check (✓) next to them. Explain your reasons to a partner.

.... a cut finger   .... a substitute teacher   .... a rainstorm

.... a camping tent   .... a vacation   .... a street name

.... a headache   .... a shoe size   .... a hobby

Literally, *ultimate* refers to the last or final thing. More commonly, it is used to indicate an extreme, such as the best or worst. *Ultimately* can mean "finally" or "basically."

*For me, the **ultimate** vacation is two weeks aboard a luxury cruise ship.*

*We tried to fix it several different ways but **ultimately** decided to buy a new one.*

B. With a partner, think of different ways to complete these sentences. Share your ideas in a small group.

1. I waited and waited for the bus to come, but ultimately . . .

2. The book I had to read for class was thick and looked boring. I started to read it. Ultimately, . . .

3. We couldn't decide where to eat dinner. He wanted to have Chinese food and I wanted seafood. Ultimately, . . .

4. My cell phone was making odd noises. I shook it and banged it on the table. Ultimately, . . .

The word *terminate* and its forms have many uses, all related to "end" or "ending."

*I **terminated** the agreement with my cell phone company because their service was bad.*

*Failure to follow the rules will result in **termination** of the game.*

*Ed was **terminated** after working for the company ten years.*

*My grandfather has **terminal** cancer.*

*Her plane arrives at **Terminal** C, Gate 7, at 7:36 P.M.*

*Each office had forty or more computer **terminals**.*

Note: *terminate* cannot be used in place of *ultimate*.

C. Match each sentence on the left with the one that explains it on the right. Compare answers with a partner.

.... 1. Alan terminated the lease on his apartment.   **a.** He fired her.

.... 2. Alan terminated Linda, his secretary.   **b.** He was fired.

.... 3. Alan's uncle has a terminal illness.   **c.** He hung up.

.... 4. Alan was terminated.   **d.** He wanted to take a bus.

.... 5. Alan waited at the downtown terminal.   **e.** He is very ill.

.... 6. Alan spent hours at his desk terminal.   **f.** He's moving soon.

.... 7. Alan terminated the phone conversation.   **g.** He used his computer.

A *trace* is evidence that something happened or existed.

> *I could see **traces** of mice in the garage.*

A *trace* is also a small bit of something.

> *The river had **trace** amounts of toxic substances in it.*

To *trace* something is to follow its history or development. Not everything is *traceable*. Sometimes records are lost or unknown.

> *The book **traced** the history of deep-sea exploration.*

> *Scientists **traced** the oil spill to a small tanker in the North Sea.*

Another meaning for *trace* is to copy the outlines of a diagram or picture.

> *He put a piece of paper over the picture and carefully **traced** its shape.*

D. Match the person on the right with the kind of tracing he or she might do on the left. Compare answers with a partner.

.... **1.** trace a picture   **a.** the police

.... **2.** trace a family's history   **b.** the post office

.... **3.** trace letters of the alphabet   **c.** a scientist

.... **4.** trace the owner of an abandoned car   **d.** a family member

.... **5.** trace a lost package   **e.** an artist

.... **6.** trace the life cycle of a butterfly   **f.** a small child

STEP II VOCABULARY ACTIVITIES: Sentence Level

The word *conduct* has different meanings in its noun and verb forms.

As a verb, *conduct* (pronounced con-DUCT) refers to something that you organize and carry out. It can also mean to lead an activity or group. This meaning has no other word forms.

> *Scientists **conducted** several underwater experiments.*

> *The team leader **conducted** most of the investigation.*

Many activities occur with this verb. For example, a person can conduct

an experiment	an investigation	a test	a meeting
an orchestra	a class	a tour	a search
a survey	a demonstration	a project	a religious service

The noun (pronounced CON-duct) is a more formal word for *behavior*.

> *The soldier received a medal for his brave **conduct.***

E. Match the people in the first column with an activity in the second column and the purpose or topic of their activity in the third column. Write complete sentences in your notebook using different forms of the verb _conduct_.

A visiting professor conducted a class on the future of sea exploration.

1. a visiting professor   a survey   playing his Symphony in F
2. detectives   a class   for the missing murder weapon
3. marketers   an experiment   to identify future customers
4. a famous composer   a search   the future of sea exploration
5. ocean scientists   a local orchestra   on poisonous algae

Word Form Chart			
Noun	Verb	Adjective	Adverb
occupancy occupant	occupy	occupied occupying	....
occupation	....	occupational	occupationally

The word _occupy_ has several meanings.

To have possession of a particular physical space:

    *The **occupants** of both apartments are gone all day.*

    *Hotel rates are based on double **occupancy** of the rooms.*

To fill a space, a period of time, or one's thoughts:

    *Studying **occupied** my weekends until I graduated.*

Politically, to take over a country or area by force and run it:

    *A foreign army once **occupied** this country. The **occupation** began in 1850.*

The noun form _occupation_ refers to the work that a person does.

    *Everyone in my family has the same **occupation**—we're all farmers.*

    *A police officer has to face many **occupational** hazards.*

If something is _occupied_, it is in use. If a person is _occupied_, then she is busy.

    *The bathroom was **occupied**, so I waited my turn.*

    *I am **occupied** all day with meetings.*

F. What are some occupational hazards for these jobs? Write one or two sentences for each occupation in which you explain some of its hazards. Discuss your sentences in a small group.

1. police officer   4. teacher   7. zookeeper
2. firefighter   5. trash collector   8. flight attendant
3. nurse   6. bus driver   9. cook

> *Process* refers to change. A *process* can refer to a natural event that occurs in gradual steps or a series of actions directed toward a particular result.
>
> > The **process** of tree growth can be traced through its rings.
> >
> > How did an author ever write a book without a word **processor**?
> >
> > From the **processing** plant, the **processed** fish is transported to markets.
>
> *Process* can also refer to checking information, fees, or other materials submitted in order to achieve something.
>
> > The university **processes** thousands of applications for admission.
>
> The phrase *in the process* can suggest two different ideas. In one context, it means a person has started a complex procedure but has not completed it yet.
>
> > Helen is **in the process** of finishing her essay for her college application.
>
> In other contexts, it describes how one action results in something unexpected.
>
> > I was cooking dinner, and **in the process** I burned my thumb.

G. Restate these sentences in your notebook to include the form of *process* in parentheses. Be prepared to read your sentences aloud and discuss them in a small group.

1. Scientists observed how vents are formed. (*the process of*)

   Scientists observed the process of vent formation.

2. Vents are formed when seawater seeps down into the earth's crust. (*the process of . . . begins*)

3. The seawater is heated to over 750° F. As it heats, it expands. (*in the process*)

4. As it rises through the cracks, the hot water dissolves chemicals from the rock. (*in the process of*)

5. Some of the minerals harden and form a rim around the vent. (*in the process*)

6. Over time, this happens again and again until a tall chimney forms. (*the process*)

H. Self-Assessment Review: Go back to page 113 and reassess your knowledge of the target vocabulary. How has your understanding of the words changed? What words do you feel most comfortable with now?

WRITING AND DISCUSSION TOPICS

1. Why do so many people in the world depend on fish as a major part of their diet? Can anything be done to change this?

2. Describe some of the ways that oceans are used for recreation. Which of these would be affected by a depletion of sea life?

3. One result of global warming is that the polar ice will melt. What other effects are possible? How will they affect the world?

4. Some people have suggested a connection between the life forms near undersea vents and possible life on other planets. Describe the connection.

GIVING NATURE A HAND

In this unit, you will

- read about old and new ways to help people overcome disabilities.
- learn to distinguish fact from opinion in your reading.
- increase your understanding of the target academic words for this unit:

advocate	discriminate	impose	proportion	tense
alternative	error	incentive	sum	voluntary
confine	evaluate	objective	suspend	

SELF-ASSESSMENT OF TARGET WORDS

Think carefully about how well you know each target word in this unit. Then, write it in the appropriate column in the chart.

I have never seen the word before.	I have seen the word but am not sure what it means.	I understand the word when I see or hear it in a sentence.	I have tried to use this word, but I am not sure I am using it correctly.	I use the word with confidence in either speaking *or* writing.	I use the word with confidence, both in speaking *and* writing.

BEFORE YOU READ

Read these questions. Discuss your answers in a small group.

1. How many people do you know who wear glasses? What would their lives be like if they didn't own a pair of glasses?

2. What does it mean to "give someone a hand"? What are some ways that people give nature a hand by keeping themselves healthy?

3. How has science helped people have healthier bodies?

READ

This article highlights some of the ways that humans have managed to overcome the obstacles that nature put it their way.

Giving Nature a Hand

For most of human history, humans have had to live with the body that nature gave them. They lacked the knowledge to improve eyes that couldn't see clearly, or help ears that
5 couldn't hear. Such disabilities were more than an inconvenience for early humans; they were a threat to their existence. A person with impaired vision might not be able to hunt or work with tools, for example. Over time, the **incentive** to
10 survive led people to develop devices that would fix the **errors** in their own bodies.

During his 12th century travels through China, Marco Polo supposedly saw people using eyeglasses. Soon, eyeglasses came into common
15 use in Italy. The **objective** of the earliest lenses was to help people see things that were close up so they could do tasks like carving or sewing. Soon after, lenses to help people see distant objects became common. In the 18th century,
20 the two types of lenses were combined in one pair of bifocal lenses so individuals who were both farsighted and nearsighted needed just one pair of eyeglasses.

Early glasses were held in the hand or clipped
25 on the nose, held there by the **tension** of the stiff wire they were made from. Modern framed glasses, **suspended** from the ears by earpieces, were uncommon until the 19th century. Nowadays, other options are available but
30 still not widely used. Only a small **proportion** (about 2%) of people worldwide who need vision correction opt for contact lenses, which lie on the surface of the eye. Fortunately, corneal implants and laser surgery may soon eliminate
35 the need for corrective devices altogether.

No evidence exists of an early device to enhance hearing, but it probably did exist. It was likely a hollow, cone-shaped animal horn with the point cut off. Held with the tip by the ear,
40 the horn could be directed toward a voice, for example, so sound waves from the voice could be focused into the ear.

An early hearing aid

In the 20th century, battery-operated hearing aids became common. The components included a case that contained a battery and a sound-amplification device. A wire attached the device to a disc that was inserted into the ear. Today, thanks to electronics, tiny devices that fit behind the ear contain both energy cells and amplifier. They provide not only better amplification, but also better **discrimination** between various sounds. There is now a surgical **alternative** to improve hearing without an external device. A medical **evaluation** can determine whether this alternative—a cochlear implant—might be right for someone with a hearing loss.

Tooth loss was common among our early ancestors due to accidents, infection, and disease. Being toothless affected people's ability to eat and speak clearly. It also made them physically unattractive. The earliest known false teeth, or dentures, date from the 15th century, when rich people were willing to spend a large **sum** of money for uncomfortable false teeth carved from ivory, animal teeth, or wood. When the process of making rubber was perfected in 1851, dentists immediately **advocated** its use as a base material for dentures. It was soft, so it would be comfortable. It could be molded to fit individual mouths, and it could securely hold artificial teeth. It was also cheap, making dentures affordable to everyone.

Today, dental implantation is available for people who need to replace one or several teeth. Fixed into the jawbone with a titanium screw, an implanted tooth becomes a permanent replacement rather than a removable dental device.

The exploration of an ancient Mayan burial site in Honduras uncovered the tomb of a young woman, **confined** there for 1,400 years. Her jawbone contained three tooth-shaped pieces of seashell embedded into the bone in spots where three of her natural teeth were missing. Was the dental implant a punishment **imposed** on her, or was it a **voluntary** procedure? Were the Mayans the first humans to give nature a hand with dental implants?

READING COMPREHENSION

Mark each statement as *T* (True) or *F* (False) according to the information in Reading 1. Use your dictionary to check the meaning of new words.

.... **1.** Survival is a strong incentive to fix nature's errors.

.... **2.** The objective of the earliest eyeglasses was to help people do close-up tasks.

.... **3.** Early eyeglasses were secured to the ears by tension.

.... **4.** A large proportion of people are choosing to have corneal implants to eliminate the need for corrective devices.

.... **5.** A penalty was imposed on people for using animal horns as hearing aids.

.... **6.** A medical examination may determine that a person's hearing would improve with a cochlear implant.

.... **7.** Better sound discrimination is possible in modern hearing aids, thanks to electronics.

.... **8.** Dentists advocate the use of dental implants as an alternative to dentures.

READING STRATEGY: Fact versus Opinion

As you read, it is important to recognize the difference between a *fact* and an *opinion*.

Fact   information that can be proven to be right or wrong.

Opinion   a statement that you cannot prove to be either right or wrong.

Opinions often contain value words such as *best, worst, beautiful, awful, funniest,* or *most interesting*. Compare these two statements:

It is raining. The weather is awful.

You can prove the first statement by looking out of the window. The second statement is someone's opinion of the weather, so you cannot prove it is right or wrong.

A. Read these statements. Decide whether each one is a fact or an opinion. Write *Fact* or *Opinion* on the line. Compare answers with a partner.

Fact **1.** Mount Everest is the tallest mountain in the world.

.... **2.** Italy is beautiful in the summer.

.... **3.** Japanese is a difficult language.

.... **4.** Madagascar is larger than Great Britain.

.... **5.** 98% of Antarctica is covered with ice.

.... **6.** Spain is more interesting to visit than Portugal.

B. Write two facts about your school. Write two opinions about your school. Read your sentences aloud in a small group and let the others decide which are facts and which are opinions. Discuss any statements that you disagree about.

C. Look again at Reading 1. Scan the article to find one sentence that states an opinion. (Hint: It's about dentures.)

STEP I VOCABULARY ACTIVITIES: Word Level

A. Match each game with its objective. Then, tell a partner how the two ideas are related.

.... **1.** soccer   **a.** to hit a ball over a net

.... **2.** basketball   **b.** to throw a ball into a hoop

.... **3.** bowling   **c.** to hit a ball into a hole

.... **4.** golf   **d.** to knock down pins with a ball

.... **5.** tennis   **e.** to kick a ball into a goal

The adjective *objective* is related to facts and opinions. A text or observation is considered objective if it only deals with information that is based on facts, not emotions. The opposite is *subjective*, meaning based on personal opinions.

Objective   *It is raining.*   Subjective   *The weather is awful.*

Objectivity is the noun form and *objectively* is the adverb form.

*Readers sometimes question the **objectivity** of a news article.*

*Newspapers try to report the news **objectively**, without personal opinion.*

The noun *objective* has a different meaning. It is a formal alternative for *goal* or *aim*.

*The inventor's **objective** was to create contact lenses for animals.*

B. Read these sentences. Cross out subjective words so that the statements become objective reports of news events.

1. The ~~beloved~~ prime minister gave a ~~brilliant~~ 30-minute speech yesterday.

2. ~~I'm angry that~~ taxpayers will face yet another large, unwelcome tax increase.

3. The audience applauded wildly after the best performance I've ever seen.

4. Two sweet children from a terrible family were found sleeping in the park.

5. I'm happy to report that the awful man got what he deserved and was arrested.

C. Read this paragraph about ways of straightening teeth. Use the target vocabulary in the box to complete the sentences. Compare results with a partner.

advocate	impose	proportion
alternative	incentive	tense
confined	objective	voluntarily

Nowadays, many adults .... the discomfort of dental braces
(1. *force*)
on themselves .... It will be the second time around for a large
(2. *willingly*)
.... of adults who are considering braces. One day they notice
(3. *part*)
that teeth which were perfectly aligned in childhood have shifted and may even
overlap. Dentists .... braces for them. Their ....
(4. *recommend*)   (5. *goal*)
is to prevent future health problems. However, the patients' ....
(6. *motive*)
is usually to improve their appearance. Standard braces are made of steel, but
a popular .... for adults are clear plastic bands. The first few
(7. *choice*)
days with new braces are the worst. The pain in their mouth makes patients feel
.... Often the pain is not .... to the mouth.
(8. *tight*)   (9. *limited*)
Patients may temporarily experience headaches and earaches, too. When the braces
are removed, most adults say that the discomfort was worth it.

Tension refers to how tightly something is stretched. It can describe the forces acting on objects or the emotional forces acting on people.

*The dentist increases the **tension** in my braces a little more each week.*

*Don's been so **tense** since he lost his job. He's been having **tension** headaches.*

*The atmosphere was **tense** as the doctor removed the bandages from his eyes.*

In grammar, *tense* refers to the form of a verb.

*The past **tense** of "keep" is "kept."*

D. With a partner, think of things that might make these people feel tense. What is the cause of the tension?

1. someone getting on an airplane
2. the hostess of a large party
3. the coach of a basketball team
4. someone going to a job interview
5. an actor in a big, new play
6. a new parent

E. An *incentive* is something that encourages a person to do something. Match the incentive with the action that will make it possible. Compare answers with a partner.

.... 1. having a nice smile
.... 2. being able to see clearly
.... 3. being able to hear conversations
.... 4. being able to eat comfortably
.... 5. having big muscles
.... 6. looking good in a swimsuit

a. getting dentures
b. lifting weights every day
c. getting braces
d. losing some weight
e. wearing a hearing aid
f. wearing glasses

STEP II VOCABULARY ACTIVITIES: Sentence Level

The word *sum* has several uses, all related to the idea of a total amount of something. In math, for example, the *sum* is the result you get when you add numbers together.

*The **sum** of 6 + 2 + 3 is 11.*

It is also the total value of a group of things.

*A team is only as good as the **sum** of its players.*

It can refer to an amount of money.

*He brought a large **sum** with him in case he had to buy dinner.*

The phrase *sum up* means to state the main points of a text or conversation.

*The doctor **summed up** the situation in three words: "You need glasses."*

A **summation** is a formal review of the main points of something, either written or spoken.

*The lawyer's **summation** of the facts of the case put the jury to sleep.*

F. Look again at Reading 1. Put a check (✓) next to the statement that accurately sums up each of these paragraphs.

Paragraph 2

.... **1.** Some people cannot see things at a distance.

.... **2.** Certain lenses are for farsighted people.

.... **3.** The history of eyeglasses began many centuries ago.

Paragraph 3

.... **1.** Modern ways to correct vision are different from earlier ways.

.... **2.** About 2% of people who have impaired vision wear contact lenses.

.... **3.** After the 19th century, glasses had earpieces to hold them on.

Now, write statements that sum up these paragraphs. Use *in summation* or *to sum up* in each statement.

   1. Paragraph 4: *To sum up, effective hearing devices didn't become available until the 20th century.*

   2. Paragraph 5: ....

   ....

   3. Paragraph 6: ....

   ....

To *impose* something <u>on</u> a person is to use authority to require them to obey. *Imposition* is the noun form.

   *The city will **impose** a fine <u>on residents</u> who park in the streets overnight.*

If someone *imposes on* you, they interrupt your routine and expect a favor from you.

   *I know it's an **imposition**, but may I use your computer?*

Someone who is *imposing* is impressive in appearance or behavior and seems powerful.

   *Standing before the crowd in full uniform, the general was an **imposing** figure.*

G. Look at the chart of things that different people might impose on others. Think of two other things for each category. Then, choose one of the sets and write a letter to a friend describing the new rules.

A Teacher	Parents	A School Campus
a no-talking rule	a midnight curfew	parking restrictions

The word *discriminate* has several different meanings related to the idea of differentiation—or noticing differences between things.

> The law should not **discriminate** between famous and ordinary people.

> Mrs. Clifford is very **discriminating**. She only serves the best quality foods.

To *discriminate* one thing <u>from</u> another means to be able to see, hear, smell, touch, or feel the difference.

> I can't **discriminate** one perfume from another. They all smell the same to me.

> He lacks the **discrimination** to tell lime green from olive green.

To *discriminate* <u>against</u> a person or a group of people is to treat them unfairly.

> In past decades, employers often **discriminated** against women.

> Racial **discrimination** is still common in many places.

It is often difficult to tell which meaning of *discriminate* or *discrimination* is being used. Here are some helpful hints.

When *discriminate* or *discrimination* means "to recognize differences,"
- it is nearly always used with *between* or with *from*.
- two or more similar things are mentioned.

When *discriminate* or *discrimination* means "to treat people unfairly,"
- it is nearly always used with *against*.
- a particular person or a group of people is mentioned.
- a particular type of discrimination is named: for example, *age discrimination*.

H. Rewrite these sentences in your notebook to include a form of *discriminate*. Read your sentences in a small group. Did you convey the correct meaning in each of your sentences?

1. Society is unfair to people who are fat.
2. People who are colorblind usually cannot tell red from green.
3. It is against the law for employers to treat someone unfairly because of his race.
4. Immigrants often face unfair treatment in their new countries.
5. Movie actors wear contact lenses because studios won't hire actors who wear glasses.
6. Lemons and limes taste the same to me.

BEFORE YOU READ

Read these questions. Discuss your answers in a small group.

1. Eyeglasses, hearing aids, and false teeth are common devices that assist people who have physical limitations. What other devices do you know of that help people's bodies function?

2. Have you ever seen people with artificial arms or legs? What could they do?

3. How do you think artificial limbs will change in the future?

READ

The title of this article refers to a 1970s science fiction television series, "The Six Million Dollar Man." In the show, an astronaut has a terrible accident. The government gives him high-tech artificial arms and legs to replace his damaged ones, a process costing six million dollars. These changes make him part human and part machine, or "bionic."

Bionic People

Some 30 years after TV's bionic man, a real bionic man has been created—and for a **sum** nearly as great. He can't run 60 miles an hour, but he does have a bionic arm to replace one he lost in an accident. This new arm is not science fiction. It is the world's first thought-controlled artificial arm.

In 2001, Jesse Sullivan was 54 years old and working as a lineman for an electrical power company. Somehow, he made an error and contacted with a live wire on the ground that gave him a 7,200-volt shock of electricity. His arms were destroyed.

After recovering from the accident, Jesse got a set of artificial arms. He controlled them by moving his back muscles and pressing tabs with his neck. He learned quickly and did well, so his doctors at the Rehabilitation Institute of Chicago advocated using him as a research subject. He would continue to use a conventional artificial right arm, but his new left arm would be a 12-pound Neuro-Controlled Bionic Arm. Instead of using his body to move it, he would use his brain.

Jesse underwent surgery to prepare for this. The objective was to isolate the healthy nerves that once controlled movement in Jesse's left arm. These nerves were reattached to muscles in Jesse's chest. Eventually the re-routed nerves would grow into the chest muscles. Finally, electrodes were attached to Jesse's chest and connected to his artificial arm. Now, when Jesse tenses these chest muscles, it creates a tiny electrical signal. The signal activates a computer in the left arm that does what Jesse's brain tells it to do. The movement is as voluntary and as immediate as it would be in a healthy arm.

The brain not only gives signals to the missing arm, it receives them as well. When a doctor touches Jesse's chest in various spots, it feels to Jesse as if the doctor is touching his thumb, for instance, even though his hand and arm are missing. Eventually he will be able to feel what the bionic hand is touching and to discriminate between sensations of heat and cold.

This bionic arm is suspended from a plastic framework that fits around Jesse's upper body. It has six motors and consists of parts from around the world. The hand was made in China, the wrist in Germany, and the shoulder in Scotland. The six motors move the bionic

arm's shoulder, elbow, and hand in unison[1]. Jesse
uses his arm to help him put on socks, shave, eat,
and do other personal and household chores just
by thinking about them.

In 2004, Claudia Mitchell became the second
person to use a thought-controlled artificial arm.
That year the 24-year-old woman lost her right
arm in a motorcycle accident. While she was
recovering from her accident, she worried about
her future. She was very brave. She did not want
the accident to impose restrictions on her or
confine her to her house. She saw no alternatives
until she read a magazine article about Jesse
Sullivan and his bionic arm. The article gave her
the incentive to try to get her own bionic arm.
She said to herself, "I've got to have one of those."

Her doctors evaluated her and agreed to make
her into a bionic woman. After surgery, Claudia
was fitted with a 10-pound artificial arm that
she controls with her brain. She has mastered
the use of her new arm and is looking forward to
entering college soon.

[1] *in unison*: together; as one

Claudia Mitchell and her bionic arm

Today a disproportionate amount of research
into brain-controlled artificial arms is focused
on implanting sensors in the brain to link the
brain to the arm. Dr. Todd Kuiken, who heads
the neural engineering program at the Chicago
Institute, rejects this approach. He says of the
technique used with Jesse and Claudia, "The
exciting thing about this technique is we are not
implanting anything into (the) body."

READING COMPREHENSION

Mark each statement as *T* (True) or *F* (False) according to the information in Reading 2. Use your
dictionary to check the meaning of new words.

.... **1.** Jesse's doctors made an error and charged him a sum of six million dollars.

.... **2.** The objective of Jesse's surgery was to isolate the healthy nerves that once
controlled the left arm and reattach them to chest muscles.

.... **3.** When Jesse tenses the chest muscles, it activates a computer.

.... **4.** Someday Jesse's hand will be able to discriminate between heat and cold.

.... **5.** Claudia worried that her accident might impose restrictions on her life or
confine her to her house.

.... **6.** She saw an alternative when she read about Jesse in a magazine article.

.... **7.** The article gave Claudia the incentive to meet Jesse Sullivan.

.... **8.** A disproportionate amount of research is focused on bionic arms.

READING STRATEGY

A. Read these statements. Decide whether each one is a fact or an opinion. Write *Fact* **or** *Opinion* **on the line. Compare answers with a partner.**

.... **1.** "The Six Million Dollar Man" was a science-fiction TV show.

.... **2.** *Bionic* is a confusing term for people with artificial limbs.

.... **3.** It must be strange to have someone touch your chest and feel it in your hand.

.... **4.** Doctors evaluated Claudia and gave their opinions about her chances for success.

.... **5.** Dr. Kuiken feels that there is a disproportionate amount of research on sensors.

B. Look again at Reading 2. Scan the article to find one sentence that states an opinion. (Hint: It's about Claudia.)

C. Write two facts and two opinions about the people in Reading 2. Read your sentences aloud in a small group and let the others decide which are facts and which are opinions. Discuss any statements that you disagree about.

STEP I VOCABULARY ACTIVITIES: Word Level

A. With a partner, list some alternatives for these situations. Which alternative do you prefer?

1. Your car is not working and you have school tomorrow. How can you get there?
2. You and a friend want to go out for dinner. Where can you go?
3. Your mother has a birthday coming up. What can you give her as a present?
4. Your family is coming to visit you at school. You live in a dorm and have a roommate. Where can they stay?

B. *Confine* **can mean to keep someone or something in a particular place. It can also refer to controlling or setting the limits of something. With a partner, match the type of business in the first column to what it confined (center column) and the kind of limit (last column). Then, tell a partner how the ideas relate to each other.**

This restaurant confined its menu to Mexican food.

1. ~~a restaurant~~	its broadcasting	girls under 18
2. a library	its children's books	~~Mexican food~~
3. a private school	its repairs	900 words
4. a clothing store	~~its menu~~	items under $20
5. an auto repair shop	its articles	Japanese cars
6. a radio station	its student body	a cozy corner
7. a magazine	merchandise	ten hours a day

> *Voluntary* describes an action that is done willingly, without being required to do it. The adverb form is *voluntarily*.
>
> *Involvement in the study is strictly **voluntary**. You don't have to do it to graduate.*
>
> *They **voluntarily** donated their time to help the researchers.*
>
> The noun and the verb have the same form: *volunteer*.
>
> ***Volunteers** at the local hospital play games with the sick children.*
>
> *Amy always **volunteers** to help out when they are shorthanded.*

C. Which of these actions do you think are voluntary? Which are required? Discuss your choices with a partner. Which would you do voluntarily?

1. giving up your seat on the bus for an old person
2. traveling to your girlfriend/boyfriend's home to meet her/his parents
3. helping clean up the area around your residence
4. getting a passport to travel overseas
5. bringing something with you when you are invited to someone's home (e.g., flowers)
6. answering questions in class
7. cleaning your apartment or room
8. participating in medical research, if you're eligible

Word Form Chart			
Noun	Verb	Adjective	Adverb
advocate (person) advocacy	advocate	....	....

D. Imagine that the city wants to build a new hospital. They asked doctors at the current hospital to volunteer ideas for the new hospital. Each doctor is an advocate for his or her own specialty. With a partner, match the doctor with what he or she might advocate. Check your dictionary for the meaning of new words.

___ 1. pediatrician   **a.** doubling the number of operating rooms

___ 2. pharmacist   **b.** installing reclining chairs for new mothers

___ 3. obstetrician   **c.** building a modern kitchen for the cafeteria

___ 4. nutritionist   **d.** building a playroom for the sick kids

___ 5. surgeon   **e.** purchasing new x-ray machines

___ 6. radiologist   **f.** adding computers to keep track of medicines

STEP II VOCABULARY ACTIVITIES: Sentence Level

> To *suspend* <u>something</u> means to hang something, either permanently or temporarily.
>
> *Jesse's new <u>arm</u> was **suspended** from his shoulder by a plastic frame.*
>
> To *suspend* <u>an activity</u> is to stop it temporarily.
>
> *The lab will **suspend** <u>research</u> on the vaccine until a new director is hired.*
>
> To *suspend* <u>a person</u> is to dismiss them from a job, school, project, etc. temporarily, usually as a punishment. *Suspension* is the noun form.
>
> *<u>Hannah</u> was **suspended** from school for a week for bad behavior.*
>
> *During her **suspension** she wasn't allowed to watch TV or go online.*

E. Rewrite these sentences using a form of *suspend*. Discuss your sentences in a small group.

1. The boss dismissed our lab technician for a week for being careless.
2. He will not be paid during the time he is out.
3. Our school will not have classes during the summer.
4. Electrical wires were strung from the power poles.
5. To save space, they are going to hang their bikes from the ceiling.
6. The moon looked like it was in the sky right over my house.

Word Form Chart			
Noun	Verb	Adjective	Adverb
proportion	....	(dis)proportional (dis)proportionate	(dis)proportionally (dis)proportionately

> A *proportion* is concerned with the relationship among the parts that make up a whole. Like a ratio, it can compare one part to another part in terms of number. It can also compare parts in terms of importance, size, degree, or other factors.
>
> *The largest **proportion** of undergraduates is made up of women.*
>
> The two adjective forms are interchangeable, as are the two adverb forms.
>
> *An enormous TV took up a **disproportionally** large area of the room.*
>
> *Each roommate had a **proportionate** amount of space in the closet.*
>
> When two parts are *in proportion*, this means they are of the correct sizes relative to each other. For instance, in an accurate drawing of a person, the ears will be larger than the eyes—but they are supposed to be. *Out of proportion* is the opposite.
>
> *The artist has drawn the eyes and ears **in proportion**.*
>
> *But look how big the mouth is. It's **out of proportion** to the rest of the head.*

F. In your notebook, restate the information using a form of *proportion*. Compare only their relative size or importance (no statistics necessary). Be prepared to read aloud and discuss your sentences in a small group.

1. The oceans of the world occupy over 70% of the earth's surface.

   The oceans of the world occupy a large proportion of the earth's surface.

2. Food from the sea provides between 5% and 10% of the total world food supply.

3. Of the earth's 6.5 billion people, over one billion rely on fish as a primary source of protein.

4. Ambition seems to coincide most often with middle-class status.

5. Celebrities as a group are more narcissistic than other people.

6. Kids with autism are predominantly male, with boys outnumbering girls by a ratio of 4 to 1.

7. About 60% of the world's malaria cases occur in sub-Saharan Africa.

8. As the rainforest disappears, so will the native people.

9. Hundreds of new gas stations were built along the highways, complemented by new fast-food restaurants.

10. Fast-Food Franchises in 2005: McDonald's 22,435; Burger King 9,944.

G. Self-Assessment Review: Go back to page 127 and reassess your knowledge of the target vocabulary. How has your understanding of the words changed? What words do you feel most comfortable with now?

WRITING AND DISCUSSION TOPICS

1. Some people consider eyeglasses one of the most important inventions in human history. Do you agree or disagree? Why?

2. What are some of the drawbacks of wearing glasses? Do contact lenses eliminate these? What problems do contact lenses cause?

3. What devices do you know of that assist people who are blind? What devices do you know of that assist people who are deaf?

4. Why did so many people from past centuries have dental problems? How does this compare to today?

5. It is estimated that Claudia's bionic arm cost $4 million. Do you think this is a good investment for research dollars? Why or why not?

Inside Reading 1

The Academic Word List
(words targeted in Level 1 are bold)

Word	Sublist	Location	Word	Sublist	Location	Word	Sublist	Location
abandon	8	**L1, U7**	**attain**	9	**L1, U5**	complex	2	L4, U2
abstract	6	L3, U5	attitude	4	L4, U6	component	3	L4, U3
academy	5	L3, U1	attribute	4	L3, U10	compound	5	L4, U6
access	4	**L1, U2**	author	6	L2, U4	comprehensive	7	L2, U7
accommodate	9	L2, U7	**authority**	1	**L1, U6**	comprise	7	L4, U9
accompany	8	**L1, U2**	automate	8	L3, U6	compute	2	L4, U8
accumulate	8	L2, U4	available	1	L3, U5	conceive	10	L4, U10
accurate	6	L4, U6	**aware**	5	**L1, U5**	concentrate	4	L3, U8
achieve	2	L4, U1				concept	1	L3, U1
acknowledge	6	**L1, U7**	behalf	9	L3, U9	**conclude**	2	**L1, U6**
acquire	2	**L1, U4**	benefit	1	L4, U2	concurrent	9	L4, U5
adapt	7	L4, U7	bias	8	L4, U8	**conduct**	2	**L1, U9**
adequate	4	L2, U4	bond	6	L4, U3	confer	4	L4, U4
adjacent	10	L2, U3	brief	6	L3, U6	**confine**	9	**L1, U10**
adjust	5	L4, U3	bulk	9	L4, U9	confirm	7	L4, U10
administrate	2	**L1, U3**				**conflict**	5	**L1, U2**
adult	7	L3, U6	**capable**	6	**L1, U8**	conform	8	L4, U7
advocate	7	**L1, U10**	capacity	5	L4, U9	consent	3	L4, U7
affect	2	L2, U6	category	2	L4, U5	consequent	2	L2, U3
aggregate	6	**L1, U9**	cease	9	L4, U10	considerable	3	L3, U8
aid	7	L2, U7	challenge	5	L3, U8	consist	1	L4, U2, U9
albeit	10	**L1, U7**	**channel**	7	**L1, U3**	constant	3	L4, U8
allocate	6	L2, U6	chapter	2	L3, U7	**constitute**	1	**L1, U4**
alter	5	**L1, U1**	chart	8	L3, U10	**constrain**	3	**L1, U8**
alternative	3	**L1, U10**	chemical	7	L2, U10	construct	2	L3, U1
ambiguous	8	**L1, U4**	circumstance	3	L2, U10	**consult**	5	**L1, U6**
amend	5	L2, U9	cite	6	L4, U10	consume	2	L2, U2
analogy	9	**L1, U4**	**civil**	4	**L1, U4**	contact	5	L2, U10
analyze	1	L2, U3	clarify	8	L4, U8	**contemporary**	8	**L1, U7**
annual	4	**L1, U9**	classic	7	L3, U9	**context**	1	**L1, U4**
anticipate	9	L2, U3	clause	5	L2, U8	contract	1	L3, U9
apparent	4	L2, U9	code	4	L4, U9	contradict	8	L2, U2
append	8	L2, U10	coherent	9	L2, U5	**contrary**	7	**L1, U6**
appreciate	8	L3, U5	**coincide**	9	**L1, U5**	**contrast**	4	**L1, U7**
approach	1	L3, U1	collapse	10	L4, U10	**contribute**	3	**L1, U9**
appropriate	2	**L1, U8**	**colleague**	10	**L1, U5**	controversy	9	L2, U3
approximate	4	L3, U4	commence	9	L3, U9	**convene**	3	**L1, U4**
arbitrary	8	L2, U8	comment	3	L3, U3	converse	9	L2, U8
area	1	L4, U1	commission	2	L3, U9	convert	7	L2, U2
aspect	2	L3, U4	commit	4	L2, U6	**convince**	10	**L1, U3**
assemble	10	L3, U10	commodity	8	L4, U6	**cooperate**	6	**L1, U2**
assess	1	**L1, U8**	communicate	4	L3, U2	coordinate	3	L2, U6
assign	6	L2, U9	community	2	L2, U7	core	3	L2, U5
assist	2	L2, U5	**compatible**	9	**L1, U9**	corporate	3	L2, U2
assume	1	L2, U1	compensate	3	L3, U4	correspond	3	L3, U9
assure	9	L3, U4	compile	10	L2, U6	couple	7	L3, U1
attach	6	L3, U7	**complement**	8	**L1, U7**	create	1	L2, U1

Word	Sublist	Location
credit	2	L3, U6
criteria	3	L3, U3
crucial	8	L3, U10
culture	2	L4, U10
currency	8	L3, U9
cycle	4	L4, U5
data	1	L2, U3
debate	4	L2, U4
decade	**7**	**L1, U7**
decline	**5**	**L1, U2**
deduce	3	L4, U7
define	1	L3, U2
definite	7	L3, U4
demonstrate	**3**	**L1, U5**
denote	8	L4, U6
deny	7	L4, U10
depress	10	L2, U4
derive	1	L4, U10
design	**2**	**L1, U1**
despite	4	L3, U2
detect	**8**	**L1, U6**
deviate	8	L2, U8
device	9	L2, U3
devote	9	L3, U9
differentiate	**7**	**L1, U4**
dimension	4	L4, U5
diminish	9	L4, U4
discrete	5	L2, U6
discriminate	**6**	**L1, U10**
displace	8	L2, U7
display	6	L3, U5
dispose	7	L4, U6
distinct	2	L3, U7
distort	9	L3, U6
distribute	1	L4, U8
diverse	6	L2, U8
document	3	L4, U9
domain	6	L2, U8
domestic	**4**	**L1, U3**
dominate	**3**	**L1, U5**
draft	5	L3, U6
drama	8	L3, U5
duration	9	L4, U1
dynamic	**7**	**L1, U5**
economy	**1**	**L1, U7**
edit	6	L4, U8
element	2	L4, U1
eliminate	7	L2, U9
emerge	4	L2, U1
emphasis	3	L2, U9
empirical	7	L3, U4

Word	Sublist	Location
enable	5	L3, U10
encounter	10	L3, U5
energy	5	L2, U5
enforce	5	L4, U7
enhance	6	L3, U1
enormous	10	L3, U8
ensure	3	L2, U5
entity	5	L4, U5
environment	1	L2, U1; L3, U8
equate	2	L2, U2
equip	7	L2, U3
equivalent	5	L3, U10
erode	**9**	**L1, U9**
error	**4**	**L1, U10**
establish	**1**	**L1, U6**
estate	6	L4, U6
estimate	1	L2, U10
ethic	9	L2, U9
ethnic	4	L2, U1; L3, U3
evaluate	**2**	**L1, U10**
eventual	8	L4, U3
evident	1	L4, U2
evolve	5	L2, U7
exceed	6	L4, U1
exclude	3	L4, U7
exhibit	8	L2, U5
expand	**5**	**L1, U7**
expert	6	L3, U8
explicit	**6**	**L1, U3**
exploit	**8**	**L1, U5**
export	**1**	**L1, U3**
expose	5	L3, U5
external	5	L2, U10
extract	7	L3, U2
facilitate	5	L4, U1
factor	1	L3, U8
feature	2	L4, U1
federal	6	L2, U3
fee	**6**	**L1, U1**
file	7	L4, U6
final	2	L4, U3
finance	1	L2, U2
finite	**7**	**L1, U9**
flexible	6	L3, U9
fluctuate	8	L2, U7
focus	2	L3, U8
format	9	L4, U8
formula	1	L4, U8
forthcoming	10	L4, U3

Word	Sublist	Location
found	9	L4, U8
foundation	7	L4, U4
framework	**3**	**L1, U1**
function	1	L3, U1
fund	3	L3, U3
fundamental	5	L4, U4
furthermore	6	L4, U9
gender	6	L2, U8
generate	**5**	**L1, U5**
generation	**5**	**L1, U7**
globe	7	L3, U2
goal	4	L3, U3
grade	**7**	**L1, U7**
grant	4	L2, U9
guarantee	7	L2, U8
guideline	8	L3, U3
hence	4	L3, U5
hierarchy	7	L3, U4
highlight	8	L4, U3
hypothesis	4	L4, U7
identical	7	L4, U5
identify	1	L4, U2
ideology	7	L4, U6
ignorance	6	L2, U9
illustrate	3	L4, U9
image	5	L3, U5
immigrate	3	L2, U1
impact	**2**	**L1, U9**
implement	**4**	**L1, U2**
implicate	4	L4, U7
implicit	**8**	**L1, U3**
imply	3	L4, U7
impose	**4**	**L1, U10**
incentive	**6**	**L1, U10**
incidence	6	L3, U10
incline	**10**	**L1, U7**
income	**1**	**L1, U3**
incorporate	6	L4, U4
index	**6**	**L1, U4**
indicate	1	L2, U4
individual	**1**	**L1, U1**
induce	8	L3, U7
inevitable	8	L2, U8
infer	**7**	**L1, U8**
infrastructure	8	L4, U6
inherent	**9**	**L1, U1**
inhibit	**6**	**L1, U5**
initial	3	L3, U7
initiate	6	L2, U10
injure	**2**	**L1, U1**

Word	Sublist	Location	Word	Sublist	Location	Word	Sublist	Location
innovate	7	**L1, U3**	mechanism	4	L3, U9	**participate**	2	**L1, U8**
input	6	L3, U6	**media**	7	**L1, U5**	partner	3	L3, U1
insert	7	L2, U9	mediate	9	L4, U2	passive	9	L2, U8
insight	9	L3, U7	medical	5	**L1, U2**	perceive	2	L2, U9
inspect	8	L3, U3	medium	9	L2, U2	percent	1	L2, U10
instance	3	**L1, U6**	mental	5	L2, U6	period	1	L2, U6
institute	2	L2, U8	method	1	L4, U9	persist	10	L2, U4
instruct	6	L4, U2	migrate	6	L3, U2	perspective	5	L3, U2
integral	9	**L1, U4**	**military**	9	**L1, U4**	**phase**	4	**L1, U8**
integrate	4	L2, U7	minimal	9	L2, U10	phenomenon	7	L2, U5
integrity	10	L3, U7	**minimize**	8	**L1, U1**	philosophy	3	L4, U5
intelligence	6	L3, U8	minimum	6	L4, U5	physical	3	L4, U4
intense	8	**L1, U2**	**ministry**	6	**L1, U2**	plus	8	L4, U5
interact	3	**L1, U8**	minor	3	L3, U7	policy	1	L3, U3
intermediate	9	L2, U7	mode	7	L4, U7	portion	9	L3, U9
internal	4	L3, U7	modify	5	L2, U3	pose	10	L3, U1
interpret	1	L3, U3	monitor	5	L2, U3	**positive**	2	**L1, U5**
interval	6	L2, U5	**motive**	6	**L1, U6**	potential	2	L4, U8
intervene	7	L2, U8	mutual	9	L3, U3	**practitioner**	8	**L1, U2**
intrinsic	10	L4, U4				precede	6	L2, U4
invest	2	L2, U4	negate	3	L4, U2	precise	5	L3, U10
investigate	4	L4, U8	network	5	L3, U2	predict	4	L2, U1
invoke	10	**L1, U3**	neutral	6	L2, U10	**predominant**	8	**L1, U8**
involve	1	L2, U3	nevertheless	6	L4, U10	preliminary	9	L4, U1
isolate	7	L3, U4	nonetheless	10	L4, U7	presume	6	L2, U2
issue	1	L4, U2	norm	9	L4, U6	previous	2	L2, U5
item	2	L3, U10	normal	2	L3, U8;	**primary**	2	**L1, U1**
					L4, U2	prime	5	L4, U4
job	4	**L1, U1**	notion	5	L4, U9	principal	4	L4, U5
journal	2	L2, U6	notwithstanding	10	L2, U1	principle	1	L3, U9
justify	3	L2, U3	nuclear	8	L2, U7	prior	4	L3, U6
						priority	7	**L1, U2**
label	4	L2, U2	**objective**	5	**L1, U10**	proceed	1	L4, U9
labor	1	**L1, U2**	obtain	2	L3, U6	**process**	1	**L1, U9**
layer	3	L3, U4	obvious	4	L3, U7	**professional**	4	**L1, U5**
lecture	6	L4, U2	**occupy**	4	**L1, U9**	prohibit	7	L3, U10
legal	1	L2, U3	**occur**	1	**L1, U2**	project	4	L4, U4,U9
legislate	1	L3, U3	**odd**	10	**L1, U8**	promote	4	L2, U6
levy	10	L2, U9	offset	8	L4, U8	**proportion**	3	**L1, U10**
liberal	5	L2, U1	ongoing	10	L3, U3	prospect	8	L2, U6
license	5	L3, U9	option	4	L4, U7	protocol	9	L2, U4
likewise	10	L4, U5	orient	5	L2, U5	psychology	5	L4, U2
link	3	**L1, U8**	outcome	3	L3, U4	publication	7	L3, U1
locate	3	L2, U1	**output**	4	**L1, U7**	**publish**	3	**L1, U3**
logic	5	**L1, U6**	overall	4	L2, U6	purchase	2	L2, U9
			overlap	9	**L1, U7**	pursue	5	L3, U8
maintain	2	L4, U1	**overseas**	6	**L1, U1**			
major	1	L3, U2				qualitative	9	L3, U9
manipulate	8	L4, U4	**panel**	10	**L1, U6**	quote	7	L4, U10
manual	9	L3, U10	paradigm	7	L2, U6			
margin	5	L4, U3	paragraph	8	L3, U6	radical	8	L3, U4
mature	9	**L1, U8**	parallel	4	L3, U9	random	8	L2, U7
maximize	3	L2, U8	parameter	4	L4, U5	range	2	L3, U1

Word	Sublist	Location
ratio	5	**L1, U8**
rational	6	L3, U3
react	3	L2, U6
recover	6	L3, U4
refine	9	L4, U4
regime	4	L2, U10
region	2	L3, U1
register	3	L2, U2
regulate	2	L3, U6
reinforce	8	L2, U5
reject	5	**L1, U7**
relax	9	**L1, U8**
release	7	L4, U1
relevant	2	L4, U8
reluctance	10	L2, U4
rely	3	L3, U2
remove	3	L3, U2
require	1	L4, U2
research	1	L4, U2
reside	2	**L1, U2**
resolve	4	L3, U4
resource	2	L3, U8
respond	1	L4, U7
restore	8	L3, U5
restrain	9	L2, U7
restrict	2	L2, U9
retain	4	L4, U3
reveal	6	L3, U8
revenue	5	L2, U2
reverse	7	L2, U7
revise	8	L3, U6
revolution	9	**L1, U1**
rigid	9	L2, U7
role	1	**L1, U5**
route	9	L2, U5
scenario	9	L3, U7
schedule	8	L4, U9
scheme	3	L4, U3
scope	6	L4, U8
section	1	L2, U5
sector	1	**L1, U3**
secure	2	L4, U6
seek	2	L4, U3
select	2	L3, U1
sequence	3	L3, U5
series	4	L3, U5
sex	3	**L1, U3**
shift	3	L4, U9
significant	1	L3, U10
similar	1	L2, U1
simulate	7	L3, U1
site	2	**L1, U6**

Word	Sublist	Location
so-called	10	L2, U8
sole	7	L4, U1
somewhat	7	**L1, U4**
source	1	L3, U2
specific	1	**L1, U6**
specify	3	L4, U6
sphere	9	L3, U7
stable	5	L4, U5
statistic	4	L4, U7
status	4	L3, U2
straightforward	10	L3, U4
strategy	2	L2, U5
stress	4	L4, U4
structure	1	L2, U1
style	5	**L1, U4**
submit	7	L2, U9
subordinate	9	L4, U3
subsequent	4	**L1, U1**
subsidy	6	L2, U2
substitute	5	**L1, U1**
successor	7	L2, U9
sufficient	3	L2, U10
sum	4	**L1, U10**
summary	4	L2, U10
supplement	9	L4, U10
survey	2	**L1, U3**
survive	7	L3, U2
suspend	9	**L1, U10**
sustain	5	L2, U4
symbol	5	L2, U2
tape	6	**L1, U6**
target	5	L3, U10
task	3	**L1, U8**
team	9	L2, U6
technical	3	**L1, U6**
technique	3	L2, U1
technology	3	L3, U8
temporary	9	**L1, U9**
tense	8	**L1, U10**
terminate	8	**L1, U9**
text	2	L2, U4
theme	8	L2, U2
theory	1	L4, U4
thereby	8	L4, U3
thesis	7	L4, U7
topic	7	L3, U3
trace	6	**L1, U9**
tradition	2	L3, U6
transfer	2	L4, U1
transform	6	L2, U7
transit	5	L3, U5
transmit	7	L4, U4

Word	Sublist	Location
transport	6	L4, U10
trend	5	L4, U6
trigger	9	L3, U7
ultimate	7	**L1, U9**
undergo	10	L4, U1
underlie	6	L4, U6
undertake	4	L2, U3
uniform	8	L3, U1
unify	9	L4, U5
unique	7	L2, U1
utilize	6	L3, U8
valid	3	L4, U10
vary	1	L3, U10
vehicle	8	L4, U3
version	5	L3, U5
via	8	**L1, U4**
violate	9	L3, U6
virtual	8	L2, U10
visible	7	L3, U5
vision	9	L4, U3
visual	8	L3, U7
volume	3	L2, U4
voluntary	7	**L1, U10**
welfare	5	L4, U1
whereas	5	L4, U2
whereby	10	**L1, U4**
widespread	8	L4, U10